# GRAPHIC DESIGN x100

# GRAPHIC DESIGN x100

DORIAN LUCAS

BRAUN

# Contents

# Preface

by Dorian Lucas

The idea behind this very unusual book came about whilst working on previous volumes: With Swiss Design and the two Green Design books, it often occurred that all the companies involved in those books who also worked in graphic design expressed a wish to design their own layout as they were not entirely happy with our suggestions.

This is to be expected, because while they take only their own pages into consideration, we have to concentrate on the book as a whole, which leads to very different deliberations and results. During discussions about this graphic design volume, the publisher decided to allow the graphic designers themselves to present their own, individually designed pages.

Just a few "set elements" help to form each composition into book pages. From an art history point of view, what is happening here is like the reconstruction of the Temple of Solomon; but at high-speed. Different aesthetic attitudes in an extremely compact form demonstrate current styles and devise their own written descriptions. There is hardly any evidence of our set elements: our instructions is like the description of the Temple of Solomon in the Old Testament, descriptive yet also leaving room for interpretation, thus resulting in widely varying outcomes.

The first Jewish temple in Schedel's World Chronicle was a centralized space with a tower in the middle of the densely populated city, in the 17th century a city palace, in the 18th century a classic free-standing Antae Temple, in the 19th century an exuberantly decorated oriental building.

This volume is also extremely versatile, with minimal stylistic demands and just the expectation that each double page is designed as freely and imaginatively as possible. Each participant received a sample page and a written "Requirements and Layout Instructions for Graphic Design Book" that create the framework for each design. The double page was sent as a spread. Set elements included the length of the office description and the project descriptions, the size of the font for the company name and the main text, as well as the page numbers and the text at the edge of the pages - the word "chapter", which would later be exchanged for the name

# Requirements and Layout Instructions for Graphic Design Book

Please use the sample pages you have been given
Name the file either with your company name or the surname of the graphic designer
The page layouts are just a reference. You can design them as you wish

You have a double page spread and are free to present from 1–3 of your company projects on these pages.
Please do not show more than three projects and do not use more than two pages.

## Images
- Images must be high-resolution 300 dpi integrated into the layout at 100%
- Color mode: CMYK Fogra. For black and white: Dot Gain 15%
- Attention!: Images must reach at least 3 millimeters over the page edges. These will then be trimmed slightly

The images will not be edited – any color faults, grainy images, unsharp images or other defects will be taken as deliberate and will be left how they are.

Please provide the copyright information for all images. There is a field for this on the page. Please don't reposition this field; it has to stay where it is.
If this box is not needed (for example, if the photos belong to the company) then this can be deleted. In this case, the entire credit for all photos on the two-page spread will be credited to you company in the book index.

## Title
- This is the name of the company or graphic designer not the name of the project(s)
- You can chose the position, font and form but the size must stay at 40 points.
- Please write just the name, without a location or country (this should be added to the main text)

## Text
- The position, font and size of the text box can be changed however you like. The font size is set at 9 points and must remain so.
- The text should be an office bio and should not be longer than 700 characters (including spaces)
- This must include the office location, the names of company partners and their birth year.
- This text will be edited by us if we think this is necessary
- Please write in the third person (do not use I or we)
- Please do not use superlatives
- Each of the 1–3 projects presented should be accompanied by a short sentence.

- All project sentences together must not total more than 2-300 characters
- These sentences should start with the project name and completion year
- We will edit this text if we think this is necessary
- Please write in the third person (do not use I or we)
- Please do not use superlatives

The text boxes containing page numbers and office name must remain as they are on the sample pages. Please do not alter these in any way.

Please „package" the book for printing and send as an InDesign file linked with images and fonts and send in a file named with your company name (You can also send a locked PDF so that we can compare it if you like)
For the index we need a portrait image (5 x 5 cm b&w), company address and homepage.

# CHAPTER 8

# *Your Name*

CV and about your Office: malesuada augue. Ut sollicitudin, lectus id gravida tincidunt, nisl risus cursus dui, at ultrices lacus diam sed odio. In eget pede nec ligula cursus tristique. Quisque porttitor. Class aptent taciti sociosqu ad litora torquent per conubia nostra, per inceptos hymenaeos. Cras

sapien. In nisi erat, pellentesque ut, dignissim vitae, dictum non, velit. Sed arcu felis, facilisis ac, consequat a, pretium et, justo. Quisque augue mi, rutrum sit amet, hendrerit sit amet, condimentum eu, nunc. Nulla tempus vulputate dui.

a sentence about the projects: malesuada augue. Ut sollicitudin, lectus id gravida tincidunt, nisl risus cursus dui, at ultrices lacus diam sed odio. In eget pede nec ligula cursus tristique. Quisque porttitor. Class aptent taciti sociosqu ad litora torquent per conubia nostra, per inceptos hymenaeos.

of the company. The line "Photos: Courtesy of the Designers" must remain on the right side by the book spine, but could be altered in terms of content or removed entirely. Basically, the sample pages were an empty white double page spread with just three vertical lettering elements, two at the top to the outside of each page and one - which should re- main in place - lower down and positioned slightly off-center. The lettering was black. In the picture above these vertical el- ements are gray. This sample page was sent to each graphic designer as an Adobe CS6 file, accompanied by the written instructions. Fur- ther elements were also present on the sample pages that weren't really mentioned in the instruc-

tions. For example, a text box
with 40 point lettering for the
office name, a two-column text box
with 9 point lettering for the
office and project description.
The instructions specified that
these must appear on the page, but
didn't specify where they should
be positioned or how they should
be presented - apart from the font
size. Some of these elements were
positioned within and some outside
of the type area - which was not
mentioned in the instructions but
appeared on the sample pages. The
type area can be seen in a light
ocher color in the image above.
Although the treatment of these
elements was left arbitrary, many
of the graphic designers never-
theless decided to use the given
elements as they were presented on

the sample pages and also chose to use the font type used on the sample page - despite the fact that only the font size and not the font type was specified. The designers also often asked what they were allowed to change, to which we answered "everything except the rubric and the page numbers at the edges of the pages, the wording of the credit can be altered or it can be removed entirely, the office name must be written in 40 point lettering, the font used for the main office description must by 9 points and the text should not be longer than 500 characters, less text should accompany the projects." While many participants adhered to more guidelines than there actually were, others deliberately adhered to less or none of the set guidelines: office names were written using larger letting than specified, and texts were often shorter, sometimes a lot shorter. This was tolerated as artistic expression, as were texts deliberately written in the first person and not in third, as was required. We only reinstated deleted rubrics and page numbers. We later changed the color of these two elements where necessary from black to white in order to make them more readable against dark backgrounds.

The pages we received also demonstrated that not all graphic designers master the technical requirements for such a layout: a lot of images were not 300 dpi, or were embedded at over 200%; fonts were also sometimes missing. These technical problems were solved by correspondence between the designers and us. Numerous files were sent as locked print-PDFs or Target Image files (*.tif) delivered with and without layers, which made text editing and correction very difficult. In addition, over time more and more sample page formats were demanded: CS5, 4 and 3 (InDesign Markup Language *.idml), Photoshop file format with layers (*.psd), Adobe Illustrator (*.ai) and Encapsulated PostScript (*.eps) versions of CS6 files were all required; some of which were unable to include all elements of the original sample page (e.g. two-column type area). The varied demands of the graphic designers and the varying knowledge in terms of offset printing techniques can be explained by the topic field itself - graphic design is a wide field and not everyone who works within this field has worked on a book. However, it was important to us that this volume - just like the previous volumes in this series -

demonstrate the entire width and breadth of this very varied and versatile discipline. Not only the layouters, typographers, calligraphers, logo or advert designers, but rather the entire spectrum. This intention is also reinforced by the presentation of well-known companies together with new talent. In addition to distinguished logos, long-established slogans, and famous campaigns, this volume also offers new images and imagery, new image codes emerging from underground subcultures, and new font designs, although handwriting or feigned handwriting also occupy an astounding amount of space - next to individually developed typography. Such designs can be found on stationary, in books and exhibition designs, on product etiquettes, posters and placards, on stamps and skateboards. In terms of the projects chosen, this was left entirely up to the designers.

In this volume, it is not only the projects presented that are important, but rather how they are presented. The presentation is just as exciting, if not more so, than the product or project itself. The composition and design of the page is the true artistic work. Has the type area been made part of the design? Have the

unavoidable set guidelines been adhered to, or even transformed into part of the design? Has the graphic designer devised a symmetrical grid for the page or used an - even decentralized - focus for the composition. Have images been laid out over the join between the pages, do the images go right to the edges? Which compositions use colored backgrounds and which leave the background white? Where are edges and lettering aligned? And where do colors correspond and why? Which layouts use the fonts from the sample pages and which use unusually fonts and lettering? Five different types of just the Helvetica font alone were used.

This volume displays an exciting panopticum of possible graphic designs, demonstrating the whole spectrum of the discipline in the second decade of the 21st century. The widely varying compositions surprise with their stylistic choices, entertaining the reader at every turn of the page, regardless of whether they are experts or just ordinary people with an interest in the exciting and varied world of graphic design.

# Rubens Cantuni

Born in Genoa and now living in Milan (Italy) Rubens Cantuni is an illustrator / artist inspired by different passions, from Asian cultures and imagery to traditional tattoos and street art.

After his degree in Industrial Design he started working in the main advertising agency of his hometown and as a freelance illustrator. Among his clients: Nike, Hasbro, Foot Locker, BNP Paribas, WWE Magazine and a whole galaxy of average, small and independent T-shirt/fashion brands.

He exhibited in group exhibitions in Milan, Paris, Manchester, Lausanne, Berlin, Athens, Brisbane and other places worldwide. Member of the Blood Sweat Vector collective, along with the best vestor artists around he has also been featured in important graphic and digital art magazines and books.

http://tokyocandies.com

RUBENS CANTUNI

# ten_do_ten

ten_do_ten

Japanese pixel designer who connects dots to dots and design pixels.

Studied under Gento Matsumoto while attending Musashino Art University in Tokyo. Was a member of Delaware between1995-2001. Started [ten_do] web site in 2001, soon after 9.11. Works with dots as a pixel design originator, with sexy, domestic, crazy-stoic attitude, everyday. Past works include interface for cell phones, book designs, editorial works, CD sleeve designs, web designs, domestic design works, collaboration and client works and exhibitions overseas.

mini_max pixel & mini_max pixel products (mass production, making things personal)

I have designed the pixel units with the impression of max minimal some of the most.

They are pixel unit of 10x10 and 3x4 pixels.

I design the graphics on products with the impression of max in the most minimal.

Milton Glaser, Inc. was
established in 1974. The
studio produces identity
programs - including logos,
stationery, brochures, signage,
and annual reports. In the field
of environmental and interior
design, we conceptualized
and site-supervised the
fabrication of numerous
products, exhibitions, interiors
and exteriors of restaurants,
shopping malls, supermarkets,
hotels, and other retail and
commercial environments.

Milton Glaser is among the
most celebrated graphic
designers in the United States.
He has had the distinction
of one-man-shows at the
Museum of Modern Art
and the Georges Pompidou
Center. In 2009, he was
the first graphic designer
to receive the National
Medal of the Arts award.
He was selected for lifetime
achievement awards from
the Cooper Hewitt National
Design Museum (2004) and
the Fulbright Association
(2011). As a Fulbright
scholar, Glaser studied with
the painter, Giorgio Morandi
in Bologna. He co-founded
the revolutionary Push Pin
Studios in 1954 and New
York Magazine with Clay
Felker in 1968.

SVA THEATER: BAR

SVA THEATER: *FAÇADE*

HELLER: *FURNITURE POSTER*

THE HERMITAGE MUSEUM: *POST PAST EXHIBITION POSTER*

THEATER FOR A NEW AUDIENCE: *DISAPPEARING SHAKESPEARE MURAL*

SHAKESPEARE STUDIES

KIKKERLAND: *CLOCKS*

BROOKLYN BREWERY: *LABEL TRADEMARK IDENTITY*

# brandient

The Creative Partner Cristian 'Kit' Paul founded Brandient in 2002 in Bucharest, together with his two partners Aneta Bogdan and Mihai Bogdan. The brand strategy and design company, with offices in Bucharest and Singapore, delivers innovative branding solutions for emergent entrepreneurs and companies. With a proven track record in difficult markets, Brandient has a deeply rooted entrepreneurial approach: unrelenting, familiar with the ever-changing new normal, offering true, customized design solutions.

Indygen Office
Indygen School
Indygen Tribe

Indygen is a brand created for a major telecom player looking for an innovative way to build and secure a relationship with young consumers. The logo exresses the natural spontanety of the kids, and is an integral part of the typeface-based visual platform. Remarkably, Indygen SIM card comes packaged in a brand-property collectable series of urban-warrior-shaped designer toys.

# SCHAFFNER & CONZELMANN DESIGNERSFACTORY

Established as a design agency in 1976, the Designers-factory Schaffner & Conzelmann has focused on all conceivable media that can be involved in one project for almost 40 years. Communication, in the sense of a goal and success-oriented approach, and its visual implementation require a pluralistic way of thinking that is free of stylistic dogma. Today, the company comprises clearly structured departments, that serve a huge range of customer needs and allow a short and interdisciplinary way to find solutions. More than 50 customer portfolios from all sectors of the economy, public and cultural sectors are currently being taken care of by our 16 employees. Over the last decade, Schaffner & Conzelmann Designersfactory has also been awarded numerous international design prizes and has curated its own design exhibitions and congresses.

# me studio

Martin Pyper ('67) is a British designer who has lived in The Netherlands for over twenty years. He operates both inside the Dutch design scene as a local, yet he has retained the observing eye and open perspective of the foreign outsider.

Me studio's work always comprises a mix of three things: image, identity and inspiration. Projects are commissioned by a broad range of clients: from cultural clients such as theater companies, publishers and film production companies to larger brands such as The Dutch Post Office, Heineken and Nike. Me studio is best known for the poster campaign for

the Dutch National Ballet on the streets of Amsterdam since 2003.

Pyper is an avid blogger, scouting design inspiration and writing articles, which are published daily on the 'me' blog. His work has won awards such as the **Best Dutch Books,** the **Chicago International Poster Biennial** and has been added to the permanent collection of the **Stedelijk Museum** for modern art in Amsterdam.

He is also a guest teacher at various design schools, amongst which the **Design Academy Eindhoven** and has been a talent scout for the **Dutch Design Awards** since five years.

**Nomads** – visual identity (2013)

An identity for an advertising agency, based on the idea of 'tribal markings'. Coloured symbols are used to represent data about the 'tribe' members. All printed elements (business cards, posters etc.) link together to create one huge tribal pattern.

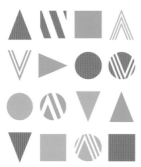

ME STUDIO

Dutch National Ballet – visual identity & campaign (2003 – 2013)

Postage stamp – Dutch Post Office (2008)

'one drop of ink can cause millions to think' – Lord Byron

# Montague Projects

Montague Projects is the solo studio practice of Julian Montague (b. 1973). Founded in Buffalo, New York in 2002, Montague Projects has been involved with a wide range of assignments for both print and web. The studio's main specialty lies in creating bold, colorful illustration based design solutions for the cultural sector. These include posters, book covers, album covers and other types of printed collateral.

*State of America* Print Series for PrintCollection.com (2012-2013). Selections from a series of posters depicting the official State insignia of all 50 U.S. states.

**Ohio**
State Reptile
**Northern Black Racer**

**Oregon**
State Fruit
**Pear**

**Arkansas**
State Mineral
**Quartz**

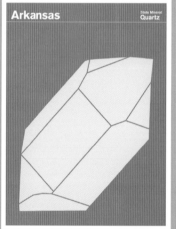

**Alaska**
State Bird
**Willow Ptarmigan**

**Rhode Island**
State Bird
**Rhode Island Red Chicken**

**Massachusetts**
State Tree
**American Elm**

# Buffalo Arts Studio presents

## April 13 2013
8 PM – 1 AM
Tri-Main Center
2495 Main Street

For one night only, 26 bands, 12 dancers and performers, 77 visual artists, comedians, and poets take over Buffalo's Tri-Main Center for WNY's biggest party to benefit Buffalo Arts Studio. Visit www.buffaloartsstudio.org for a full listing of participants.

# trimania

TICKETS: $20 advance/student ticket • $25 at the door • $75 VIP pre-party ticket includes 2 beverages and hors d'oeuvres by The Lunch Box Cafe / Credit cards accepted at the event
TICKETS AVAILABLE at www.buffaloartsstudio.org & at the following locations until Friday, April 12th: Buffalo Arts Studio • Record Theatre • Rust Belt Books • Talking Leaves...Books • Tri-Main Center • Western New York Book Arts Center
SPONSORS: WGRZ • Matt Brewing Company • Try-It Distributing • Lamar Advertising • Progressive Direct Marketing • Custom Tees • Premier Wine & Spirits • Buffalo Rising

*Trimania* poster and billboard 2013. Promotional pieces for an art event in Buffalo, New York

Series Aphonos LP designs, 2013

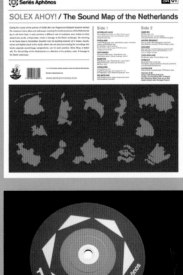

# SEAN FREEMAN •

A love of words and beautiful images led Sean Freeman to explore a harmony of both, spreading his wings to open up his own studio: THERE IS, specialising in creative typography, illustration and art direction.

Based in East London, Sean creates award winning typographic treatments and illustrations for a varied range of clients globally from advertising to music, editorial and publishing; with his work being featured in numerous books and magazines. His work is known to be as powerful as it is unique: a dynamic and organic fusion between elements.

Forever curious, Sean is constantly exploring new ways of approaching his work with a love for happy accidents and a passion for visual storytelling, texture, type and everything in between.

*Left: i; One lonesome letter from an alphabet I created in an effort to make each letter as fat & furry as possible.*

*Right: Suddenly; An alphabet created for Noteography, a tool to make type type online visually more interesting. Shot with Iain Crawford.*

*Below: ABC, A few cupcake letters from an alphabet we created for a Playstation Network campaign.*

SEAN FREEMAN

# Julene Harrison

*Originally a constructed textile designer, UK born and currently living in Chicago, Julene turned her hand to paper-cutting in 2009. The work is primarily text based but portraits and illustrations of all kinds are undertaken. Her passion for the precise and her background in the design of textile patterns have combined to make Julene's style of paper-cutting such a success.*

*The Picture of Dorian Grey. 2013 - Personal Project*
*Part of a series called 'Storytelling'. Each piece features a pivotal plot point shown in a relevant holding device. In this piece Dorian laments his inevitable ageing and wishes that his likeness in the painting would grow old, rather than he. The holding device is the frame of the painting.*

*There is a Light. 2012 - Private Commission*
*There is a Light That Never Goes Out by The Smiths.*

JULENE HARRISON

THERE IS A LIGHT
THAT NEVER GOES OUT
TAKE ME OUT TONIGHT
OH, TAKE ME ANYWHERE, I DON'T CARE
I DON'T CARE, I DON'T CARE
DRIVING IN YOUR CAR
I NEVER, NEVER WANT TO GO HOME
BECAUSE I HAVEN'T GOT ONE, NO, NO
OH, I HAVEN'T GOT ONE
AND IF A DOUBLE-DECKER BUS
CRASHES INTO US
TO DIE BY YOUR SIDE
IS SUCH A HEAVENLY
WAY TO DIE
AND IF A TEN-TON TRUCK
KILLS THE BOTH OF US
TO DIE BY YOUR SIDE
WELL, THE PLEASURE
THE PRIVILEGE IS MINE
OH, THERE IS A LIGHT
AND IT NEVER GOES OUT
THERE IS A LIGHT AND IT NEVER GOES OUT
THERE IS A LIGHT AND IT NEVER GOES OUT
THERE IS A LIGHT AND IT NEVER GOES OUT
THE SMITHS

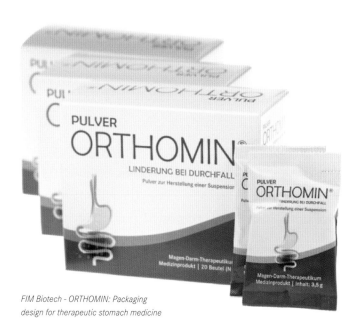

*HÈRMAN NATURKOSMETIK: Brand development - from design conception to production*

*FIM Biotech - ORTHOMIN: Packaging design for therapeutic stomach medicine*

Born in Buenos Aires and raised in South America, Michaela Prinz grew up in an international atmosphere. Berlin is the city of choice for the marketing and communication specialist. She gained a wide range of practical experience working for various advertising agencies before spending a year working in the land of her birth in 1998/99. Returning to Germany with a wealth of inspiration and experience, with energy and creativity, she began working in Berlin as a freelance graphic designer in various industries. It was during this time that she began to focus on architecture and design.

In 2010, the successful art director founded "Prinz+Partner", a network of freelance strategic designers, graphic designers and production managers. Here, specials work together in teams on specific projects, with a focus on service and reliability. The aim is to be that bit more individual, that little bit faster, and always extraordinary. This basis has resulted in the development and realization of a range of successful campaigns and advertisements

*Michaela Prinz*

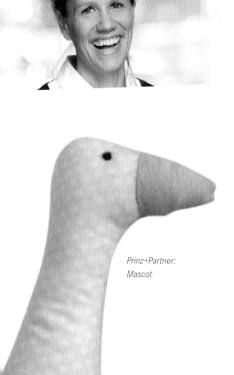

*Prinz+Partner: Mascot*

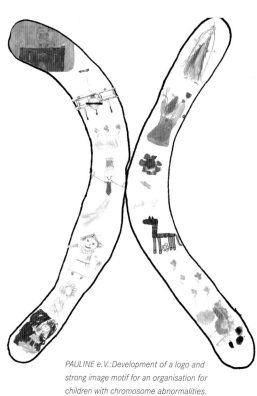

*PAULINE e.V.:Development of a logo and strong image motif for an organisation for children with chromosome abnormalities.*

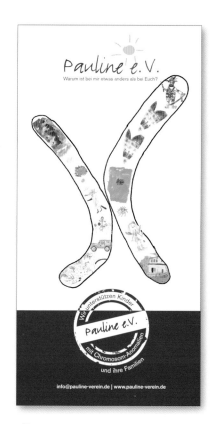

*BUWOG-Meermann – B-ZOOM: Layout concept and implementation for a magazine about Berlin's Brunnenviertel*

*BUWOG-Meermann – BUWOG TO GO!: Pocket-size trade fair flyer with flying butterflies*

*BRAUN Publishing – minimemo: Idea and design*

*BRAUN Publishing: Design concept for books, book cover and implemented layout.*

*From the many worlds that weren't simply given to human kind, but which had to be created by an individual spirit, the world of books is the largest.*

*Hermann Hesse*

Martin Schmetzer specializes in hand drawn typographic logotypes and illustrations with an emphasis on ornamentation and highly detailed flourishes. His style can range from a vintage, 1900's-era feel to a full-blown street graffiti temperament. Layers upon layers of detail add a real 3D depth to much of his work. Representation from Popill illustrator agency in Scandinavia and Red Ape in Australia/Asia.

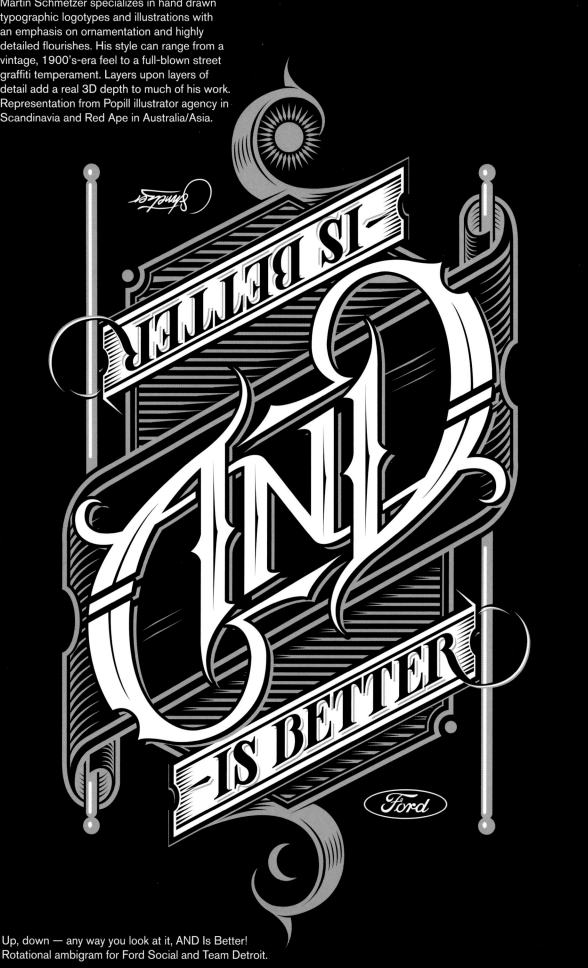

Up, down — any way you look at it, AND Is Better!
Rotational ambigram for Ford Social and Team Detroit.

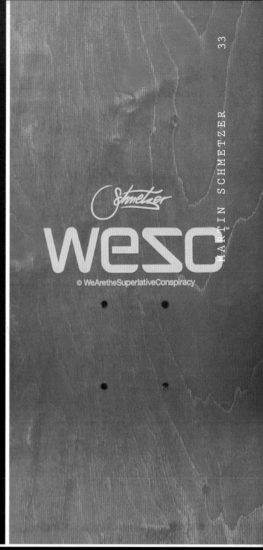

MARTIN SCHMETZER

© WeAretheSuperlativeConspiracy

Martin teamed up with WeSC, to design a limited edition t-shirt and skateboard deck graphic. Available only at the store Kungsgatan 66, Stockholm.

Photo: Niklas Skoglund

# EMEKX

Client: Edward Sharpe and the Magnetic Zeros, 2012 Silkscreen Tour Poster

Client: Coachella Music Festival, selections from 2007-2013. Silkscreen Concert Posters

WWW.EMEK.NET
Portland Oregon USA

EMEK.net

Client: Pearl Jam, 2013. Silkscreen Concert Poster

# Filip Filkovic Philatz

Filip Filkovic Philatz is a filmmaker by day and a graphic designer by night. He is the impeller of Kunstterrorist Organisation, radical art initiative for publishing visual and audio works which spawned from his provocative collaboration with legendary UK artist James Cauty (The KLF) on a series of artworks for CNPD project. He is now mostly involved in film and video production having directed a bunch of music videos and commercials. Graphic design is the basis for all his works and lately he's been transitioning to feature films with his debut feature being in pre-production phase. He is also the founder of More Magnets, production house, post production studio and all purpose navel for filmmakers and like-minded individuals. He approaches his directing work through the eye of the designer.

"As filmmaker I'm interested in pervasive figurative logic as opposed to the graphic design work where I'm constantly trying to find a dynamic link in a sensibility. These screenshots are examples of my work where I mix both worlds. I like to work on every shot both through cinematic storytelling and emotionally as graphic designer."

*Vision is the art of seeing things invisible* - Jonathan Swift.

# Sumayya Alsenan

Born in Saudi Arabia (1984), Sumayya Alsenan pursued her BA degree in Visual Communication at the American University of Sharjah, UAE. From there, Sumayya moved to New York to earn her MFA in Design from the School of Visual Arts in 2008. Since then, she has worked in various design firms in NY, such as C&G Partners, Pentagram, Siegel+Gale and others. She is currently a lecturer at Shillington School of Graphic Design.

Cat Lady Preserves
Branding and Packaging

Client:                    Cat Lady Preserves
Design/Art Direction:      Sumayya Alsenan
Year Completed:            2012

Dorito West / Saint-Etienne International Design Biennale + 2013 Juncture poster with photographer Thomas Heinser / for AIGA

# M-A-D is Erik Adigard and Patricia McShane, a brand, communication & experience design studio

launched in 1990 in San Francisco

••approach: social sciences, spatiality, temporality, technology, ethics

••commissions: Adobe, Architect magazine, Autodesk, ExperimentaDesign, Etapes magazine, HP, IBM, Microsoft, MOMA, SFMOMA, Venice Architecture Biennale, Villette Numérique, Wired, WiredDigital

••publications: History of Graphic Design, CA, Eye, Graphis, NYT, Novum, Page, Pyramyd, Thames & Hudson

••academia: California College of the Arts

••awards: AIGA, Chrysler Award for Innovation in Design, Rome Prize + nominations from NDA & McArthur Foundation

••organizations: AIGA + AGI

••more: m-a-d.com

# Luca Fontana

Luca Fontana is a young graphic designer born in Belluno, Italy. He is specializes in brand image, illustration and graphic design. In 2008 after receiving his diploma in Art direction from the Accademia di Comunicazione (Milan), he developed an eye for the typography and graphic elements and decided to become a graphic designer. From 2009-2013 he worked at BBDO in Milan as a graphic designer. He currently works as a freelancer.

—

Being a global brand means being cosistently recognizable throughout the world. A global brand creates its own world, a world with a recognizable design, with a specific vision, with a shared philosophy and with a unique experience. Luca Fontana has formalized the identity, the personality, the mood, the soul and the unique style of the new Wall Street English world.

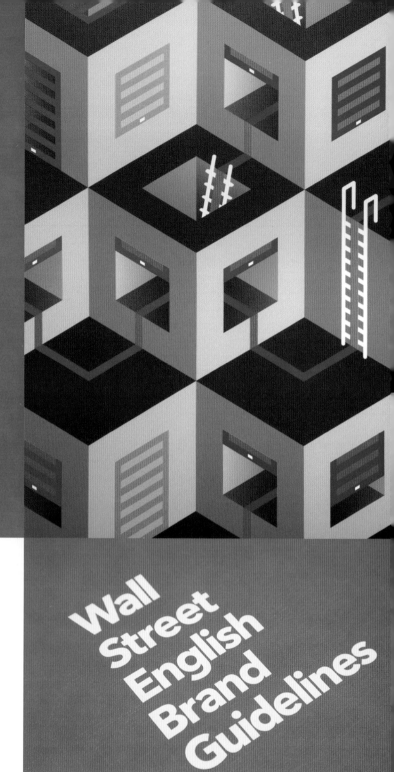

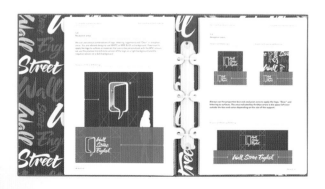

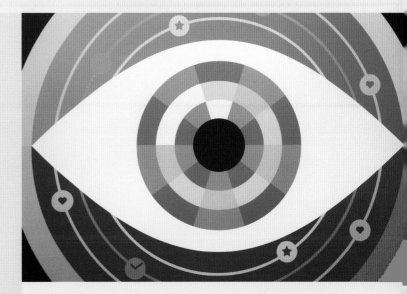

# OPÉRA[Graphiks]

Opéragraphiks™ is the studio's name of the French graffiti artist and graphic designer, Stéphane Vignal. He lives and resides in Paris. He actually does artistic direction for advertising agencies, corporate enterprises and brands. This gives him the freedom to work on more personal projects in parallel by collaborating with other artists on various projects revolving around publishing, fashion, music or video.

He now loves to play with typography, primary forms, and he is passionate about movements like Constructivism, Retro-futurism, and the Bauhaus School, which are a very deep inspiration for him.

◢ Art Direction & Illustration /2010/2013
Personal Types treatement and logotypes work

◢ Art Direction & Illustration / 2012
Personal greetings
Types treatement
3D Work by O.Regneault /// FR

◢ Art Direction & Illustration / 2012
C2C /// TETRA Album DELUXE EDITION
Types traitement for the CD booklet

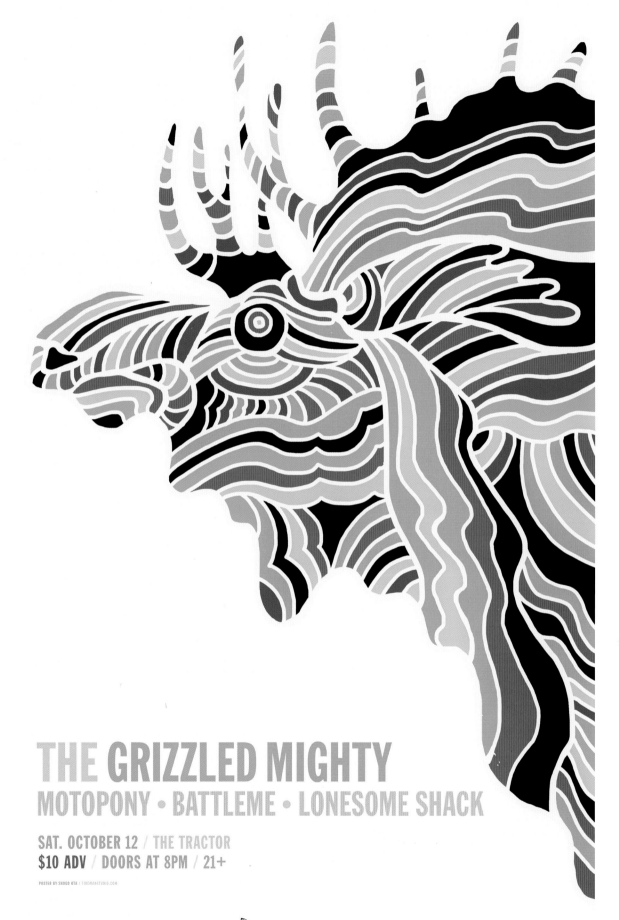

# THE GRIZZLED MIGHTY
## MOTOPONY · BATTLEME · LONESOME SHACK

**SAT. OCTOBER 12** / THE TRACTOR
**$10 ADV** / DOORS AT 8PM / 21+

POSTER BY SHOGO OTA / TIREMANSTUDIO.COM

## TIREMAN STUDIO

Tireman Studio is a Seattle, WA based graphic design
and ART company by SHOGO OTA. Keep Rolling!

TiremanStudio.com

Poster for my
Friends band
"The
Grizzled Mighty"
2013
©TMS

# *SolitaireDesign*

SolitaireDesign is a creative company that specializes in integrated visual communication. We conceive, design and create meaningful communication media using both print and digital media. Our main focus is on creating sustainable projects for a range of industries. We are committed to combining aesthetically appealing solutions with a focus on sustainable strategies and procedures - Visions of Responsibility.

www.solitairedesign.de

## visions

## *DIE ZUKUNFT, DIE ICH WILL!*

### "The future that I want!"

2013 - In what kind of world do we want to live in? SolitaireDesign brings global sustainability targets to the fore.

## spaces

# digital

## Die Biomillionen-Show & Game

2012/13 - Who wants to be a millionaire? What about bio-millionaire? This playfully raised awareness of and interest in the area of biodiversity.

# identity

DRIVING INVESTMENT IN SUSTAINABLE ENERGY

## BASE – Basel Agency for Sustainable Energy

2013 - Stong impulses for a strong concept - SolitaireDesign has developed a new corporate design for BASE.

# MIK BARO

Mik Baro (León, Spain 1978) studied Engraving and Printing Techniques at Escuela de Arte de León (1999) and graduated in Fine Arts from the Facultad de San Carlos in Valencia (2005). Beyond academics, his main visual reference materials are comics, vinyl covers, t-shirts and posters hanging on bar walls and street walls. He currently resides in Valencia where he has developed his career as a freelancer in illustration and graphic design, working overall with a dedicated passion in graphics for music. On demand by music promoters, Spanish and international music labels, and many artists themselves, he has created countless record covers, posters and merchandise designs. Over the last fifteen years, as an undeniable fan of rock'n'roll, he has been shaping graphic identities for the music and its fans.

**left:** Los Mambo Jambo" Impacto Inminente"- LP 12'' (Buenritmo-ElToro. 2013) Pájaro "Santa Leone"- LP 12'' (Happy Place. 2012)

**right:** various logos and letterings done for clients (bands, record labels, shops, clubs, rehearsal rooms) over the last years. (2009-2013)

right: "The Grekos" promotional poster for festival in southern Spain.
client: Musica Fundamental (2013)

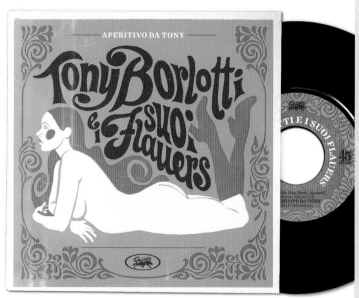

above: Tony Borlotti e i suoi Flauers "Aperitivo da Tony"- EP 7" (Discos Jaguar. 2013) Le Grand Miercoles "Comin'home baby / Alligator ye-ye"- single 7" (Rufus recordings. 2012)

**TOX.ORG**
CHEMTRAILS AWARENESS TOUR 2014

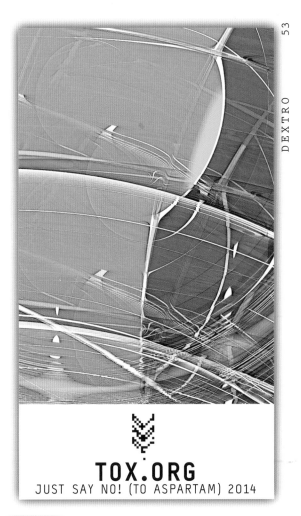

**TOX.ORG**
JUST SAY NO! (TO ASPARTAM) 2014

*dextro.org is run by vienna-/berlin-/tokyo-based dextro since 1994. it displays his non-commercial visual experiments (many code-generated), photos, videos and most recently, oil paintings.*

in this series of posters (and folders) for the alternative information site tox.org code-generated images were used, alongside photos of paintings of such images (as seen on the left). the idea was to help convey intellectually demanding information by combining it with intuitively appealing, non-objective images, the latter of which would assist the former by attenuating or drawing onto themselves adverse feelings that viewers experience when learning that their food is being poisoned, the sky above them is being sprayed with chemicals on a daily basis, and that what they believed to be an illegal drug is actually a powerful tool for coping with such disasters by providing access to deep insights and high levels of awareness and empathy. in addition to that, their hypnotic quality and lack of decodable information could (like music) open a gate to the subconscious mind through which the messages could be delivered, without being fended off by its rational counterpart. other topics were: the health hazards of smart meters and the effectiveness of vitamin b17 in preventing and curing cancer.

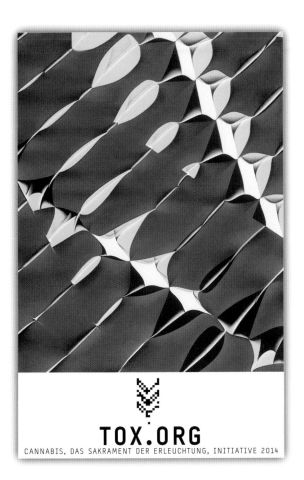

**TOX.ORG**
CANNABIS, DAS SAKRAMENT DER ERLEUCHTUNG, INITIATIVE 2014

# DEXTRO.ORG

# Bernardo **Rivavelarde**

Rivavelarde is a graphic artist. He is striving to create an artistic body of work, and bring graphic design into art, and introducing the result to the clients and viewers alike. He created Rivavelarde studio in 1997 (Madrid, Spain) with his twin brother Miguel Rivavelarde. Bernardo lives in Madrid and Gothenburg (Sweden).

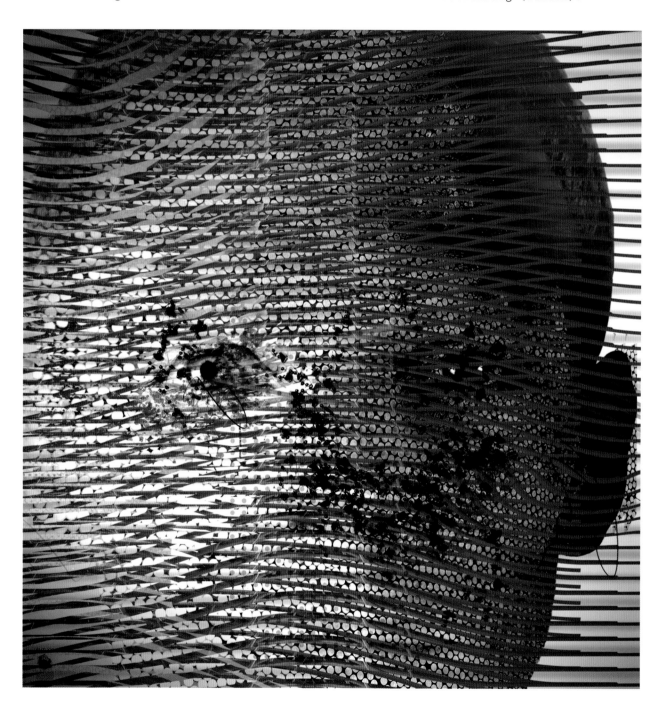

This page: Main image of Future Nature exhibition (2012)
Facing page: three more images from Future Nature, and three art works for the Zazuela Theater, Madrid (Spain).

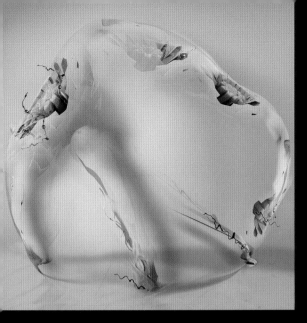

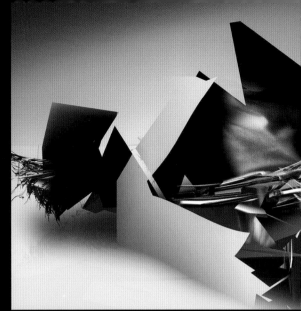

自然

CURRO
VARGAS

MÚSICA DE
RUPERTO CHAPI

ZARZUELA EN TRES ACTOS
DE JOAQUÍN DICENTA Y
ANTONIO PASO Y CANO

"DE LO HUMANO... Y LO DIVINO"

[ ANATOMÍA DE LAS PASIONES ]

TEATRO DE
LA ZARZUELA

BLACK EL PAYASO
I PAGLIACCI

# Thomas Manss & Company

www.manss.com

Alemanha + Brasil

Zal Telecomunicazioni

LA21 Landschaftsarchitektur

VCC Perfect Pictures

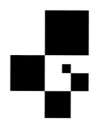

BMI Participações

Lean Alliance

Atlantic Energy

Tim Wood Furniture

Depken & Partner

Metamorphosis

Val Taylor

Transformal

'Thomas Manss & Company are designers, but they are also – and more importantly – narrators, myth-makers, fabulators and tellers of tales,' the late Conway Lloyd Morgan once described the company's multi-disciplinary design approach. With offices in London, Berlin, Cesena and Rio de Janeiro, Thomas Manss & Company helps commercial enterprises as well as cultural and government organisations to tell their story in print and online, through campaigns and exhibitions. The one visual element that unites all of these different expressions and makes them instantly recognisable is the logo – it is the peg to hang the story on.

White Biotechnology

Palazzo Avino

Meoclinic

Logistics Net

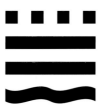

FH Brandenburg

Brainshell

Lill

Axentum

Pat Prudente

Vivité

Datatrain

UGO

# NATASCHA SAUPE KOMMUNIKATIONSDESIGN

Natascha Saupe Kommunikationsdesign is a small but successful design office that places great importance on using an integrated approach to tackle each new challenge. Founded by Natascha Saupe (*1980) in 2010, the company focuses on classic assignments, such as the development of corporate identity and editorial design. Main activities include consultation, concept, and

implementation. For every assignment, a visual concept is developed that is tailor-made to suit individual demands. Customers include commercial businesses and publishers, as well as others from the creative industries.

Sibylle Schade Coaching | 2013 | customer: Sibylle Schade | complete visual concept, implemented for office equipment and flyers

Lapp Group personnel brochures | 2012 | customer: U.I. Lapp GmbH | client: AVS Werbeagentur GmbH | complete graphic concept and design of the new personnel brochures for U.I. Lapp GmbH, Stuttgart

# leomaria design

*»Design is art that makes itself useful.«* CARLOS OBERS
Following this slogan we have been working for
various clients in corporate, editorial and web design
since 2008. Our office is based in Berlin, Germany.
The founder and creative head of the office is the
graduate designer Markus Büsges.

# numa + ático 16

**numa designs:** marta, 1983.
**ático 16:** carlos, 1983.

As freelance designers with quite different backgrounds but both with a common goal: good graphic design.
Based in London & Barcelona and working all over the globe, depending on where the clients call us.
Their style of the work pays extra attention to

typography & calligraphy, resulting in many hours fighting with the guides & alligning objects, spoiling files for every new brand in order to make it a consistent one.
Loving old school well structured brands in which every milimiter matters, rather than some tiring photoshop artwork out there.

**http://numarta.com**
**http://wwaw.atico16.com**

**kinetic body:** (2013) branding image for this training & health company. The patters illustrate different training and programmes to be followed, deppending of the kind of customer and their goals:

**th2 designs:** (2013) branding image re-design for this interior design company, which once usec to be fuchsia. Focus on the infinitive golden proportioned line in between the two letters and development of a branded heart shape based on the 2 shape.

th2

[+44] 20 7349 9494
enquiries@th2designs.co.uk
th2designs.co.uk

405 Design Centre East,
Chelsea Harbour, SW10 0XF
London

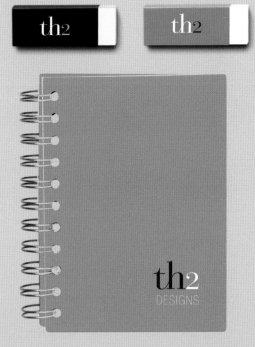

th2
DESIGNS

th2designs.co.uk
405 Design Centre East,
Chelsea Harbour, SW10 0XF
London

th2

Camille Smith
[+44] 0207 349 9494
camille@th2design.co.uk

th2designs.co.uk
405 Design Centre East,
Chelsea Harbour, SW10 0XF
London

# peter anderson studio

The team at Peter Anderson Studio strive to create innovative and thought provoking work, priding themselves on their experimental approach and curious minds. With over 15 years experience, the studio has worked across projects ranging from branding, publishing, print, sculpture and image making to titles design and in-show graphics for television and film.

1. Cayenne restaurant
2. Datavirus, Independent Newspaper
3. Ford Speak alphabet, Ford
4. In-show graphics, Sherlock, BBC1
5. Title sequence, The Shadow Line, BBC2
Background Image: Rochdale brand identity

1

2

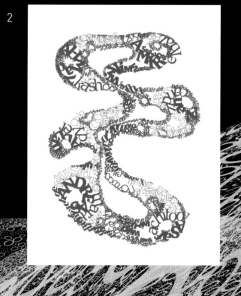

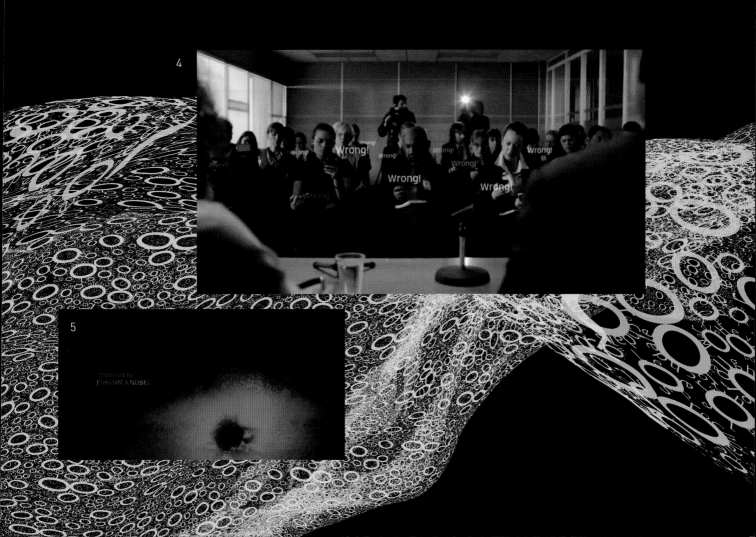

# Ougrapo

**Ougrapo** (OUvroir du design GRAphique POtentiel) **is a workshop for »graphic design under constraints«.**

**Founded in 2000 in Frankfurt / Main, Germany, by Sophie Dobrigkeit** (*1971)**, Ulrike Gauder** (*1965) **and Sigrid Ortwein** (*1965)**, this experimental group focuses on constraints and methodologies in the working process of a graphic designer.**

**Ougrapo deliberately and systematically limits itself by applying constraints to the seemingly** unlimited amount of choices and thus increases the creativity needed. Ougrapo is rooted in the domain of graphic design but often crosses the borders of the discipline.

Ougrapo invents, collects and applies rules and constraints. All of them are archived on ougrapo.de.
The output of the group is made public in books, posters, objects, lectures and workshops like the »Ougrapo Picture Wordshop«, picture-wordshop.de.

**OU LI PO OU GRA PO** / Eine Gebrauchsanweisung / book / 2013
Spreads featuring the projects »Betriebsausflug« and »Oukipo«
**OUGRAPO MANIFESTO** / poster / 2013

# Ougrapo Manifesto

**Free your mind** of the constraints
of daily routine.

**Rules are constraints** in time, space,
material, process, or behavior.

**Follow your rules** as strictly as possible.
Work hard and never stop too early.

**Chance** is not generally excluded
but must be used **consciously.**

**The focus is on the making**
not on the object.

**Forget the boundaries of your discipline.
Any material** can be the starting point of
a project.

**Make your own rules**
and use them as your **tools.**

**Don't expect. Be surprised.**

PHOTOS: Ougrapo / Ralf Barthelmes (Portrait)

© 2013 Ougrapo | Sophie Dobrigkeit | Ulrike Gauder | Sigrid Ortwein
ougrapo.de | picture-wordshop.de

# Paul Rogers

Paul Rogers is an illustrator who thinks of himself more as a graphic designer who draws as an illustrator. He often utilizes historic 20th Century visual styles and typography to making images for today's audience. He lives and works in Pasadena, California.

*This page:* Commemorative postage stamp for The United States Postal Service.

*Facing page:* Series of CD covers for Milan Music, France.

"GATSBY le MAGNIFIQUE"
Les ENFANTS du JAZZ
F.SCOTT FITZGERALD et la MUSIQUE

NINA SIMONE
COLLECTOR

BANDE ORIGINALE du film
"Le MAGICIEN d'OZ"
& les grands succès de
HAROLD ARLEN

EDDIE COCHRAN
COLLECTOR

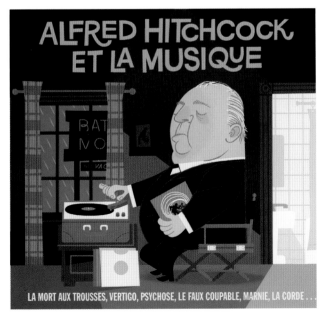

ALFRED HITCHCOCK ET LA MUSIQUE

LA MORT AUX TROUSSES, VERTIGO, PSYCHOSE, LE FAUX COUPABLE, MARNIE, LA CORDE...

FATS DOMINO
COLLECTOR

# STUBBORN SIDEBURN

**STUBBORN SIDEBURN** is a Seattle WA. (USA) based company and it was founded by **Junichi Tsuenoka** to broaden his visual communication and to employ his visual language in art, illustration, and design. Junichi Tsuneoka was born in 1975 in Japan and, upon graduating from Waseda University in Tokyo, arrived in the US at the end of the 20th Century. Junichi established a style often recognized as "**California Roll Stylie,**"

the result of both a visual and conceptual fusion of Japanese pop culture and American urban culture.

*Left: Dragonique (2011), a gallery event promotional graphic*
*Right: Steve Aoki concert poster (2013) for Sasquatch Music Festival*

# GUASH ARTS

Guash Arts is a design studio that specializes in creating graphic projects, visual identity, illustrations, visual interfaces, concepts for games and animations. The goal of the studio is to create high-quality and innovative products and services. Marco Mendonça is a designer with more than 15 years of experience and skills: He continually tries to improve all products seeing each new project as a challenge.  Versatility and quality are the words that defines Guash Arts and his team.

Branding and Creation of Mascot. The goal was give the product
a striking aesthetic appeal.

These were developed for Art&Cia School, a complete visual identity for promo with posters.

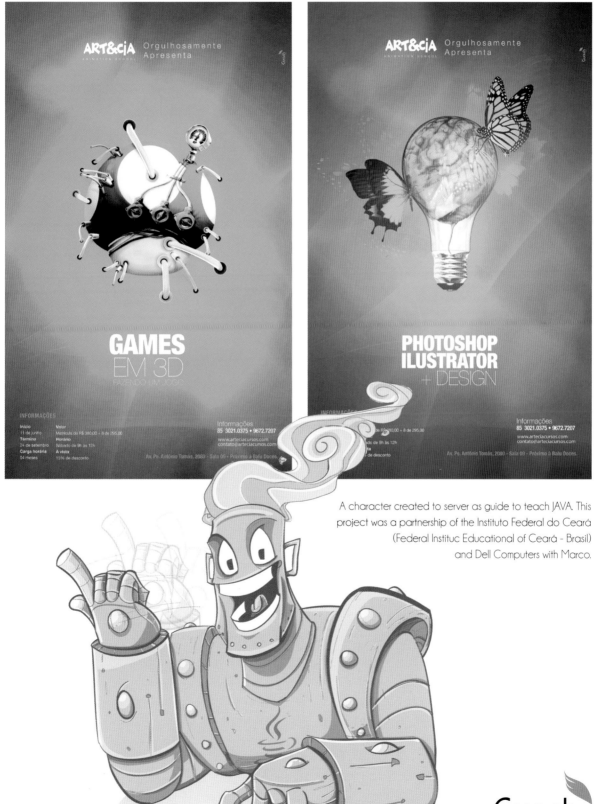

A character created to server as guide to teach JAVA. This project was a partnership of the Instituto Federal do Ceará (Federal Instituc Educational of Ceará - Brasil) and Dell Computers with Marco.

# Intergalactico

Intergalactico is a multidisciplinary art studio run by Chris & Denise Capuozzo. The studio was opened in 2008 in Chestnut Ridge, New York. Intergalactico is about establishing relationships in the world based on inspiration, exploration, discovery, and conversation. Intergalactico loves working with people who want to invent new ways of seeing and being seen.

LEFT: T-shirt illustration for Stussy, 2010.
RIGHT: Covers of CrazyGON 1, 2007 and CrazyGON 2, 2012. CrazyGON is a book series published by Intergalactico, and is an outlet for experimental work featuring work by the studio as well as other artists.

# SIMON ÅLANDER

Simon Ålander is a Swedish letterer living and working in Stockholm. He usess both analog and digital tools to create all kinds of different letterforms. All of his work is hand-drawn to give every project a unique look and feel.

"The Black Gold" is part of a series of coffee filters drawn for a guest appearance on the blog drawcoffee.com. Ink on paper filter. (2012)

Malt, Hops and Beer Styles. Lettering pieces for a book by the Scottish brewery Innis & Gunn. (2012)

Beer Styles

**VUVUZELA / 2013**
The idea for this work was simple: mixing elements of cheerleading, party and soccer in a single image. It was used to widen the campaign reach during Confederations Cup. The competition was held in Brazil in June 2013.
Agency: África - Client: Brahma

The studio started with a couple's union, Jean Campos and Patricia Palma, partners and owners of Romeu & Julieta Estúdio. Romeu has experience in fashion and advertising.
He worked as an illustrator for the fashion market, illustrating for brands like Lilica Ripilica and Marisol.
He currently serves as Dream Maker and Creative Director, working in projects for Mercedez-Benz, Starbucks, Disney, Brahma, Globo, Bradesco, and many others.

Julieta graduated in advertising and is the head of the account executive department in R&J studio, establishing a friendly contact with great advertising agencies,
making bonds with exceptional partners, and illustrating and animating dreams.
Her animations and illustrations traveled around the world through partnerships with agencies such as BBDO NY, W/McCann, AlmapBBDO, Young&Rubicam, and many others.

**MAP RS / 2012**
The purpose of "Mapa Ilustrado" of Rio Grande do Sul, a Brazilian state, was to
use local characteristics to make an image that represents landmarks and cultural
traits of each region, revamping the state's visual appeal internationally.
Agency: Escala Client: Governo do Estado do RS/SETUR

**PÃO&COMPANHIA / 2012**
The main challenge presented by this project was to design a scenario made of different kinds of bread.
The design reinforces the idea that bread is the product a bakery offers its customers.
A key focus of the concept was to communicate that all products made by the client are natural.
Client: Pão&Companhia

# Tommy Li

Tommy Li is a branding consultant for this generation renowned for his "Black Humor" and "Audacious Visual" designs. He is one of the few Hong Kong designers who can carve out a quadro-career in Hong Kong, China, Italy and Japan. Tommy stood out from other Chinese designers and received as many as awards in the 1st and 2nd International Chinese Graphic Design Competition, for being one of the most distinguished design companies. In 2007, he was presented the "Gold Pencil Award" by The One Show in New York. In 2010-2011, Tommy collaborated with Swire Properties to organise his "VISUAL DIALOGUE-Tommy Li and Works 20 Years Exhibition".

**Bla Bla Bra, 2007**
New brand identity revamp exercise including naming, logotype, visual identity, packaging, promotion material and retail shop.

**Ying Kee Tea House, 2010**
New brand image development, including logotype, visual identity and packaging.

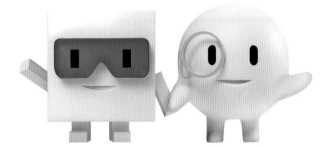

**Hong Kong Productivity Council, 2012**
Government organization image revamp including naming consulting, logotype, visual identity, mascot, packaging and animation.

# Pattern Matters

## LIM SIANG CHING

Siang Ching is a Singapore based Graphic Designer/
Illustrator. She graduated from Nanyang Academy of Fine Arts
with a Diploma in Visual Communication, and a First Class
Honors Bachelors in Design Communication from LASALLE College
of the Arts. She is the founder of Pattern Matters who finds
joy in patterns and everything handmade.

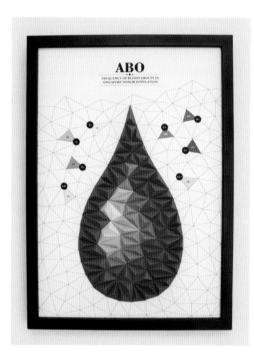
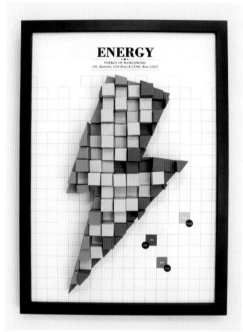
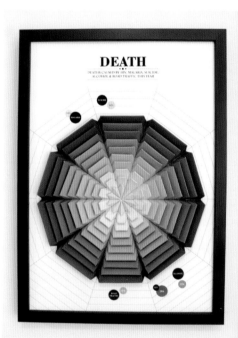

Pattern Matters is a graphic design-based project investigating on possible ways
to augment the role of pattern by looking into the design process and tactile
exploration through pattern making. It demonstrates the way of how this design
element of pattern can be adopted differently on various platforms in graphic
design. The main objective of this project is to inspire designers to look at
pattern from every possible angle. Pattern Matters also aims to demonstrate that
pattern is a crucial form of design element in graphic design and is not merely a
decorating tool.

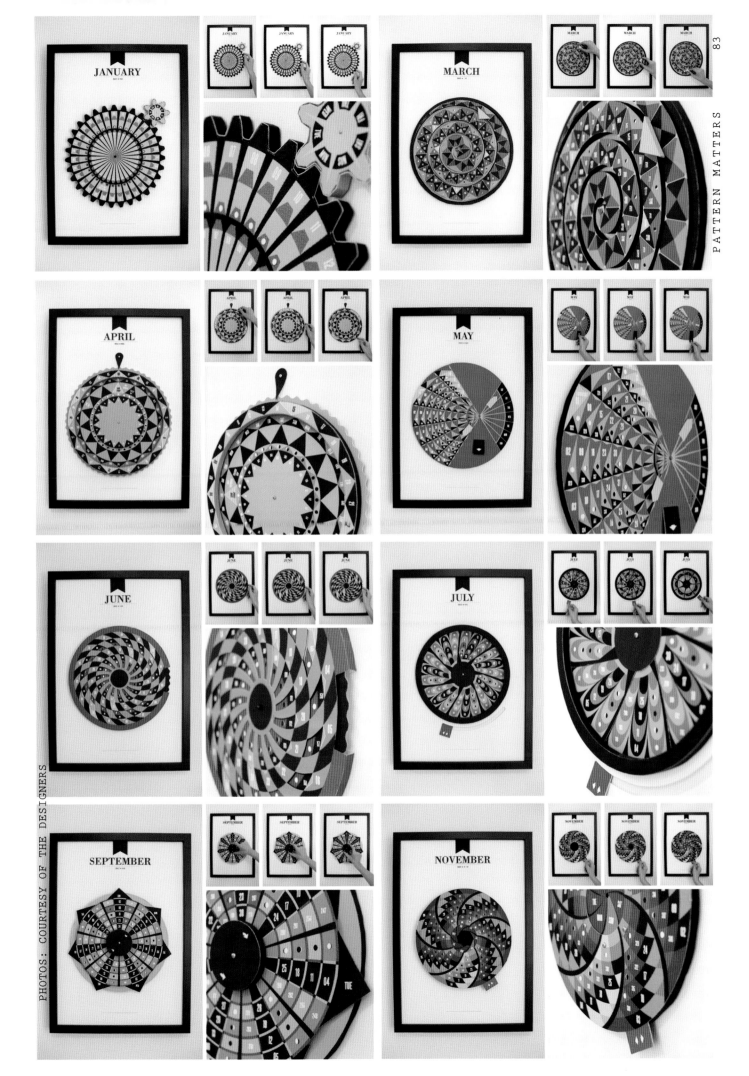

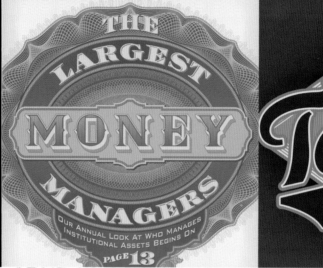

Daniel Pelavin b. 1948, maintains a studio in New York, NY. His work is best recognized for precisely drafted shapes, unique color palette, and original typography.

WANTED

CLASSIC AMERICAN SPEECHES 85

DANIEL PELAVIN

IMA 2011 SALARY SURVEY

CRÈME TRAITANTE POUR LES MAINS ET LES ONGLES

CRÈME MAINS

LA SOCIÉTÉ PARISIENNE DE SAVONS

MARQUE DÉPOSÉE

TRADE MARK

HAND CREAM

TREATMENT CREAM FOR HANDS AND NAILS

CLOUD 9

EAT HERE

30 ESSENTIAL TEXAS RESTAURANTS

2011 Data BOOK

HIGH

2012 TOP DOCS ISSUE

869 PHYSICIANS

89 MEDICAL SPECIALTIES

MORE THAN SKIN DEEP

MANAGING OUR WELL-BEING

INSIDE AND OUT

DÉCOR: LAKEFRONT MODERN

THE SEASON

Holistic Pet Care

Fall's Hottest

HURLY-BURLY

FASHION INSTITUTE of TECHNOLOGY

LIFE IN TH

NEW

# T J HAYES

T J Hayes is an independent design company, believing in strong typography & geometric design. Utilising a masculine utilitarian vibe throughout their work to achieve the most effective design solutions. Select clients include AVUND goods which is a minimalistic leather goods company combining the accuracy of modern technology with the feel of traditional crafts, as well as the likes of veren water & global edit.

For adittional information please visit www.tom-hayes.co.uk

# A.G

*"Scandinavian inspired luxury goods, designed and made to last the test of time"*

# 1295 BREWING Cᵒ

# Taxi Studio

Taxi Studio is a creative agency specialising in creating, building and activating brands. They operate across diverse global market sectors on projects ranging from snacking innovations and global spirits rebrands to corporate identities and guerilla viral stunts. The business has amassed over 130 creative honours to date and runs on three ruling principles: fearless creativity, fairness and real relationships.

www.taxistudio.co.uk

**Established:** 2002
**Location:** Bristol, UK
**Partners:** Alex Bane, Spencer Buck, Ryan Wills & Brian Mansfield

**Hudnotts: 2013**

A premium range of flavoured spirits. A brandmark crafted from a single piece of rope carries a series of eclectic illustrations based on the Seven Deadly Sins.

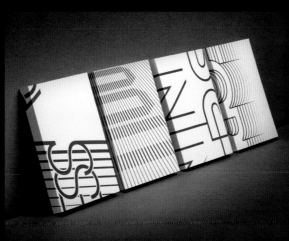

### Penstripe: 2013

A new identity system
for makers of bespoke
daily planners. Striking
line drawings serve as
a twist on the classic
British pinstripe suit.

# Christian Michel

Citizen of Mexico City, the capital of visual jam, a place full of color, techniques, visual interpretations, objects and messages that have used to instill the capacity to create monsters capable of riding bikes with their eyes closed.

Born in 1975 with the mission of launching Infección Visual. Graphic designer, creative director and illustrator. His work explores extraordinary situations with special characters that come alive in a Kids' Biker Clothing line.

"The Block Rockin' Beasts".

# Boglárka Nádi

I was born in Székesfehérvár, on a sunshiny day in 1989. I've always been interested in drawing, I went to elementary school in my hometown, and continued my art studies in high school taking drawing lessons and attending graphic design class. After that, I started university at the Institution of Applied Arts in Sopron. I have studied there ever since, in an inspiring atmosphere, along with wonderful people.
I get inspiration from my environment, from everything that I see and like. I graduated in 2012 with a stamp collection about hungarian folk tales and do have a favour for stamp design since then. After that I applied to do my Master of Arts at to the same school and will graduate next year. What wil happen afterwards? I don't really know, I'll go with the flow.

Hungary is well-known for it's traditional, beautiful, ornamental embroidery styles. In the past decade folk art has become very popular amongst young designers world wide, despite the fact that it requires a lot of creativity, hard work and research to make something new out of it.
I developed an interest in ornamental design, which became close to my heart and has had a great influence on my recent work. I can mostly describe my work with one word "elaboration", I like how the wonders of the world and mysteries are hidden in the small details.
I often use folk tale themes, traditional flowers and insanely detailed ornamental patterns.

# DARREL REES

Darrel Rees has been working as an illustrator since leaving the Royal College of Art in London in 1987. He has worked for a broad spectrum of clients across a variety of subject matter and applications. He founded the Heart Agency in 1994 and the New York sister agency Heart USA Inc in 2001, which represent some of the most influential contemporary illustrators working today. He has contributed to various publications and his book, "How to be an Illustrator" published by Lawrence King Publishing has been translated into several languages. He lives and works in London and New York. www.heartagency.com

**Observer Life Magazine**
Yeltsin

**The Telegraph**
Growth/New Technology

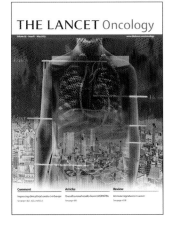

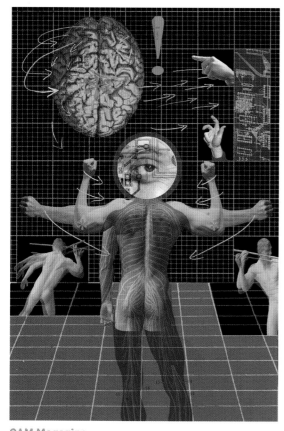

**CAM Magazine**
Memory

**New Scientist**
Chaotic Brain

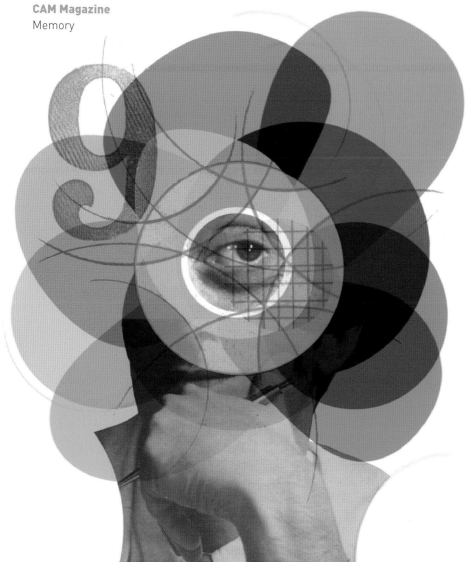

Stanford Social Innovations Review

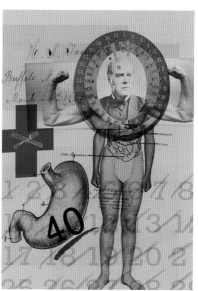

**Harpers Magazine**
Starve Yourself to Vigour

# TOBIAS GEYE

Born in Bavaria, Germany, in 1974, Tobias Geye is a Southern California graphic designer and artist whose work is a thematic collision of hot rods, rockabilly music, comics, B movies, and pulp novels. Based in Long Beach, California, he is responsible for creating key art for numerous bands such as the Stray Cats, Social Distortion, Sublime, and the Offspring, as well as works for Harley-Davidson, Dodge, and other prominent car culture icons. He was the official artist of the Toyota Grand Prix of Long Beach in 2011 and his work was featured on the #38 cover of DICE Magazine. His art and design is on a range of products, including apparel, posters, books, and throughout the motorsports world.

Ink-n-Iron Kustom Culture Festival (2009-Present)
Key art, marketing, and collectible merchandise.

Hootenanny Music Festival (2001-Present)
Key art, marketing, and merchandise.

97

TOBIAS GEYE

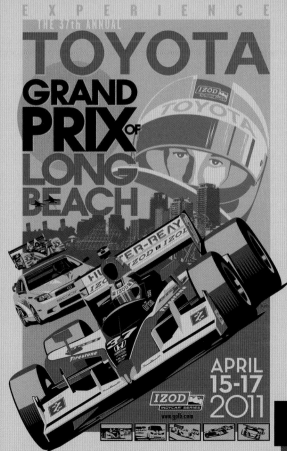

Toyota Grand Prix of Long Beach (2011)
Key art and comprehensive advertising.

# JIANI LU

Born in 1991, Jiani Lu is a young graphic designer from Toronto, Canada. Growing up, she was inspired by visits to art galleries and museums that lead to a passion for doodling, paper cut-outs and origami from a young age. Over the years, the hands-on experience in design and crafts has translated into a key interest in print design, book binding, sewing and paper crafts. She responds to spontaneity and experimentation in her work process; embracing new mediums, materials and formats at every opportunity.

Since 2013, Jiani works as a graphic designer at Slash: Creative Solutions in Dubai.

**VISUAL LANGUAGE**

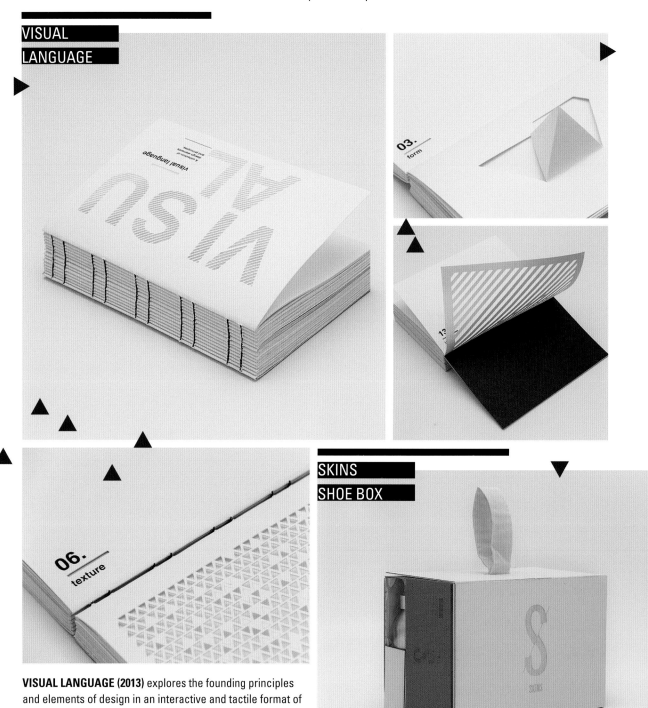

**SKINS SHOE BOX**

**VISUAL LANGUAGE (2013)** explores the founding principles and elements of design in an interactive and tactile format of a hand-bound book. The project approaches each element and principle through a restricted palette while limiting itself in being expressed solely through elementary shapes and forms.

**SKINS SHOE BOX (2012)** looks at how the traditional shoe box can be repurposed into a more meaningful experience and transfer across multiple uses. The all-in-one design functions with multiple lives: a carry box, stackable shoe shelf, and fold-out hanging organizer. This extends the purpose past its initial objective of simply transporting the shoes and accessories from the store to home. **TRIANGLES AND SHIT (2013)** is a personal project exploring Japanese stab binding and hands-on print making techniques utilizing diecut stencils and metallic spray paint.

*Sevenfold 03/2013.*
*A visual identity for Sevenfold, a fashion label Joelle initiated.*
*She conceptualized the clothing line itself and created the*
*visual communication.*

# JOELLE WALL

Joelle Wall is a graphic designer from Toronto, Canada currently based in Amsterdam. Since 2008, she has used her unique illustrative style and eye for detail to create striking visual experiences across print and digital platforms. Her work has been honoured with numerous awards from FPO, The Advertising & Design Club of Canada, Graphis, RGD Ontario and the Adobe Design Achievement Awards. Joelle holds a diploma in both graphic and fashion design and often strives to find ways to merge these two disciplines.

*Personal Stationary 10/2012.*
*Business cards that combine a typographic pattern with a folded*
*stock to produce a dimensional feel.*

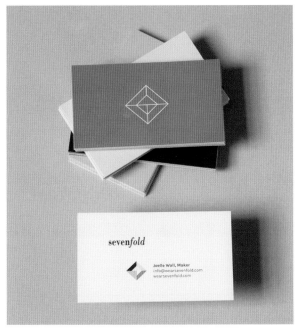

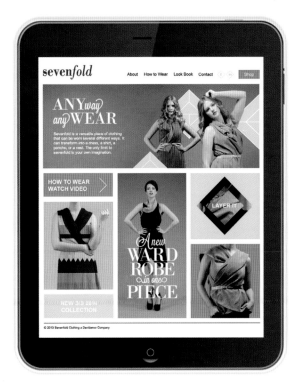

Alán Guzmán it's a mexican graphic designer, and a type and lettering lover, born in "La Heroica Guaymas and raised in Hermosillo, Sonora, México, "City of the Sun" and the beatiful womens, this dude had been working letterings since 2010 for many brands of clothes and magazines around the world, he's a very nice guy who also loves fútbol (soccer), ska music, beer, tacos, tequila, sombreros, burros, zarapes, mariachi's, you know because he's mexican, just kidding and he likes many other stuffs.

Series of letterings designed for P&G México for a Old Spice campaign called "El pueblo", the claim was "A real man is" this design is for "hairy".

ALÁN GUZMÁN

Lettering designed for the UK clothing brand "Supremebeing" in 2011 for their fall spring collection.

Part of a personal project called "Pornotypes" this one is "La Redhead" 2012.

PHOTOS: COURTESY OF THE ARTIST

# HEE RA KIM

Hee Ra Kim is a New York based graphic designer and received
BFA in Graphic Design at School of Visual Arts in 2013.

This project involved redesigning book jacekts for The Best American Series. It was
created based on an historiacal reference; a baseball ticket from 1932.

# Entire Studio

A graphic design studio run by Mattias Brodén.
Specialized in visual and corporate identities.
Our tools are brand and design strategies, design
development, packaging design, retail and digital
design. Renew & refine.

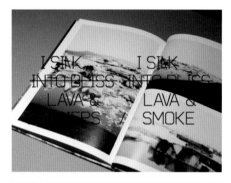
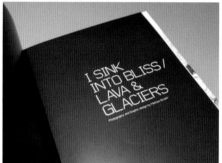
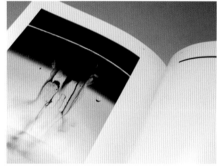

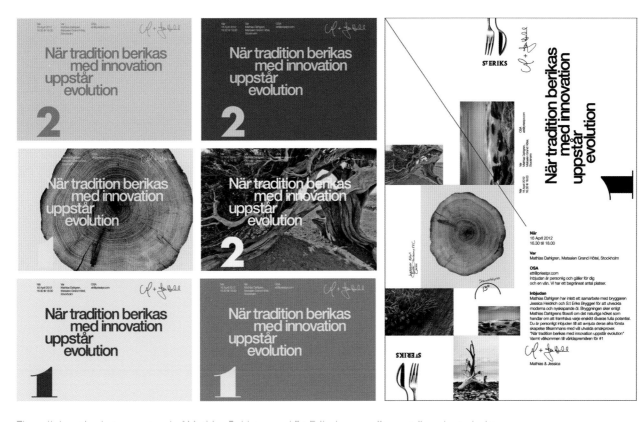

The collaboration between star chef Mathias Dahlgren and S:t Eriks brewery. Concept & package design.

# DIK &
# STIJLLOOS

met CÓLA

Dik&Stijlloos (translation: Fat & Without any style) is a young and creative designers duo from Holland. Charlotte Porskamp (1985) and Marijke Timmerman (1985) are experts in story telling and visualizations, always with a touch of analogue technique to create more depth in the stories they want to tell. This way of working results in illustrations, animations, graphics and own concepts.

SUSHI

PHOTOS: COURTESY OF THE DESIGNERS

* 'Analoque Photoshop' (2011- ) is a expanding collection of pictures Dik&Stijlloos edited by hand. Paint, pencil, scissors and glue are the most populair tools to do this. One hour without using a computer a day keeps the doctor away.

# PHILIPP ZURMÖHLE

Philipp Zurmöhle is a German Illustrator and Graphic Designer from Hannover who currently lives in Nuremberg. Philipp gained work experience at Mission Design in Oslo, where he was involved in building inspiring identities for a range of Norwegian clients. Being employed as a Graphic Designer at adidas headquarters for three years he created apparel illustrations for the global market.

His freelance design experience ranges from branding projects to illustrative work; like for example designing the new logo for the glassware brand Leonardo, apparel graphics for the kids' clothing brand Soft Gallery from Copenhagen or the creation of a complete identity for the German product design agency Ding 3000. Above: Illustrations for the local optician Herr Menig in Nuremberg, Germany.

> www.philippzm.com

## BOOK SHOP IDENTITY >

VON & ZU BUCH is a book shop for books that are especially well made. The identity for the store expresses the exclusivity of the books in an elegant way.

The horizontal line in the identity resembles the book shelves in the shop while the ampersand symbol contains the forms of the letters V and Z from the name.

## < SEVEN MONKEYS

Poster illustration with handdrawn portraits of different types of monkeys showing the seven deadly sins.

# Tobiasz Konieczny

Tobiasz Konieczny is a 24-year old Graphic Designer from Warsaw, Poland. He is a member of the American Institute of Graphic Arts. His work spans branding, illustration, and web design.

His mission is to improve the quality of life through visual communication. He strives to determine and create a unique style for each individual project he come across.

NW Studio, 2013.

NW STUDIO is owned by jewellery design student Nicole Waniowska. She gathered experience in Academy of Fine Arts, Lodz, Fachhochschule Dusseldorf and as intern in "Flux + Form" design studio and Emily Gill jewellery atelier in Toronto.

Glimm Technology, 2013.

Glimm Technology is a group of ambitious and dynamic people with a passion for technology and marketing.

Poster for Sonic Protest, Brussels, 2013

# zeloot

My favourite posters to work on are the ones where I am left completely free artistically and with which I have a strong connection concerning the advertised events, like these.

Poster for Galerie West, Den Haag, 2013

Zeloot is the pseudonym of silkscreener/ illustrator/ graphic designer Eline van Dam (1974). In 1996, she graduated from the Fine Arts department of the Royal Academy of Art in The Hague, the Netherlands (on painting). Her work mainly consists of posters for the experimental and alternative music scenes. Her designs are very much influenced by the limitations and process of silkscreening. For the last two years she has worked and lived in Gruiten, Germany. She is currently working on children picture books.

Zeloot drukt bij de Grafische Werkplaats !!

Poster for Grafische werkplaats, Den Haag, 2012

# HIDEKI NAKAJIMA
## NAKAJIMA DESIGN

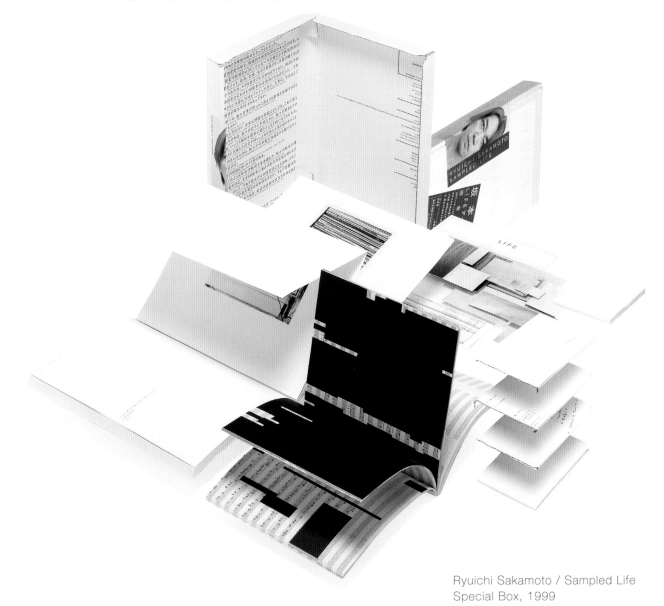

Ryuichi Sakamoto / Sampled Life
Special Box, 1999

**Hideki Nakajima Biography**
1995 Established NAKAJIMA
DESIGN inc.
HP: www.nkjm-d.com
Mail: info@nkjm-d.com
2004 Joined
POCKO,London,U.K.
2008 Joined G/P GALLERY,
Tokyo, Japan

**Awards**
1998–2001 The Art Directors
Club Awards, 5 Golds, 8 Silvers
1999 Tokyo Art Directors Club
2001–2009 The Chicago
Athenaeum's Good Design
Award
2006 The 51st Type Directors

Awards N.Y.
The Tokyo type Directors Club
Awards (Grand Prix Prise)
2007 The Tokyo Art Directors
Club Award (Memorial Prize of
Hiromu Hara)
2008 The Tokyo Type Directors
Club Awards

**Solo Exhibition (selection)**
2006 Clear in the Fog: Hideki
Nakajima Exhibition, ggg (ginza
graphic gallery), Tokyo Japan
2009 Collection-Nakajima,
The OCT Art & Design Gallery,
Shenzhen, China
2012 Hideki Nakajima 1992
–2012, Daiwa press, Japan

**Selected Publications**
1999 Hideki Nakajima Revival,
Tokyo, rockin'on
2002 Clear in the FOG Hideki
Nakajima, Tokyo, rockin'on
Hideki Nakajima Design, Dailan,
Dailan University of Technology
Press
2010 Street view / line Hideki
Nakajima, Tokyo, G/P Gallery
2012 Hideki Nakajima 1992
–2012, Tokyo, Daiwa press

**Member**
Alliance Graphique Internationale
The Art Directors Club
Tokyo Art Directors Club
Tokyo Type Directors Club

CUT, NO.23, Cover, 1993

Seven Exhibition, 2005

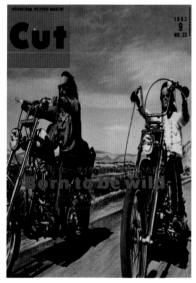

Idea, No.297, Re-Cycling, 2002

CitF_#1, 2006

CitF_#2, 2006

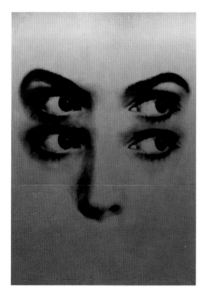

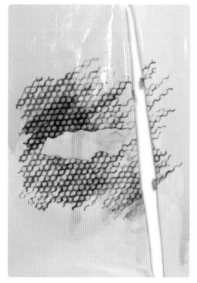

Re-CitF "Gray", 2008

Infinite Libraries, 2008

Re-Street View / Line 3, 2010

# Rian Hughes

Rian Hughes is a London-based graphic designer, illustrator, comic artist, author, and typographer. From his studio, Device, he has produced a broad selection of work across different media, including watches for Swatch, Hawaiian shirts, logo designs for *Batman* and *Spiderman*, record sleeves for Ultravox and Charlie Lankester, an iconoclastic revamp of British comics hero *Dan Dare*, and collaborated on a set of six children's books with Geri Halliwell. A retrospective monograph, *Art,* *Commercial*, was published in 2002. Recent books include *Cult-ure: Ideas can be Dangerous* and *Lifestyle Illustration of the 60s*, and his comic strips have been collected in *Yesterdays Tomorrows*. *Soho Dives, Soho Divas* is a collection of imagery inspired by London's underground burlesque scene.

1 *Archer and Armstrong* logo
2 *X-O Manowar* logo
3 Tiger Lily burlesque poster
4 Atomstile print
5 *Soho Dives, Soho Divas* book illustration
6 *Teenage Mutant Ninja Turtles* logo
7 *Batman Incorporated* logo
8 *Magical Teenage Princess* book jacket
9 *Soho Dives, Soho Divas* book illustration

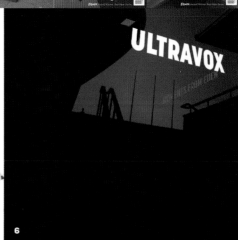

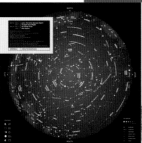

# pohl & rick
## GRAFIKDESIGN

This design agency from Düsseldorf is at home in all disciplines. For more than 15 years the two designers have been developing new visual solutions with passion and a love for detail. Be it magazines, catalogues, brochures, advertisements, websites or books – from conception and

implementation through to supervision of the printing process, everything is in the hands of the two designers. They provide a creative service that is utilized by publishing houses and creative professionals as much as by small and large companies from many different industries.

# Laura Meseguer

Laura Meseguer (b. 1968) is a freelance graphic designer, typographer and type designer based in Barcelona, Spain. She is active in the field of commercial work and personal projects. She specializes in any kind of project based on typography, from lettering for logotypes to custom typefaces and book design. She releases and promotes her typefaces through her own digital foundry, Type-Ø-Tones. In addition to her practice, Laura is a teacher of Typography and Type Design. As an author, she has published a book on the subject: TypoMag. Typography in Magazines for Index Book, and as co-author Cómo crear tipografías. Del boceto a la pantalla, published by Tipo e. She gives lectures and workshops all around the world.

**Magasin** (2013).
A display typeface inspired by the pointed pen and copperplate calligraphy, yet with a retro-chic twist. It combines a sense of script with geometric structure resulting in idiosyncratic curves softly connecting the vertical elegance of its forms.
www.type-o-tones.com

*Tipofino*

**Tipofino** (2013). Lettering for an online shop of typographic objects. www.tipofino.com

Lola Letters
Appetizer
BANGKOK

**Lola** (2013).
A display typeface with a lot of personality. www.type-o-tones.com

**Multi** (2011-2014). Custom typeface family for Dutch newspapers. Project done with Good Inc.

**Dauro** (2013). Custom typeface family for an olive oil brand. Project done with Lo Siento Studio

**Dos mil dotze punts** (2012). Poster for a 2nd year anniversary.

# HIEU TRIEU | Freelancer
Graphic Designer

I choose Graphic Design as my University course because I did not know what to do at that time. Now I really love Graphic Design. It gives me opportunities, money, reputation and even good taste.
I worked as a designer for around 4 years so I know my strengths lie within branding design, typography and printing art. I have honed my expertise from branding projects and I have learned a lot from my customers. Each project is interesting in its own way and brings its own challenges. I once worked as a designer for Haagen-Dazs for a year and began working as a freelancer in March 2013. This has helped me form my design style and develop my own customer base, as well as being involved in many interesting projects. Now I'm going to open my own graphic design studio in Vietnam. I hope I will never stop working with Graphic Design.

## PURSUE YOUR DREAM | Calendar Design

## LA VOILE SAIGON - FRANCE RESTAURANT | Brand Identity

La Voile Saigon is one of my most successful branding projects. It focuses on a French-style restaurant. The retro style logos and icons are all drawn by hand with a focus on classic imagery, but still in keeping with the original flavor of the food.

See more at:
http://www.behance.net/hieutrieu

## OTHER PROJECTS | Logo, Illustration, Packaging, Typography, ...

Vietnamese Traditional Pattern
By Hieu Trieu

SEE MORE MY PROJECTS AND CONTACT ME AT:

http://www.behance.net/hieutrieu

Web portfolio: http://hieutrieu.weebly.com

Email: hieutrieu2208@gmail.com

BÜRO FÜR FORM

# BÜRO FÜR FORM

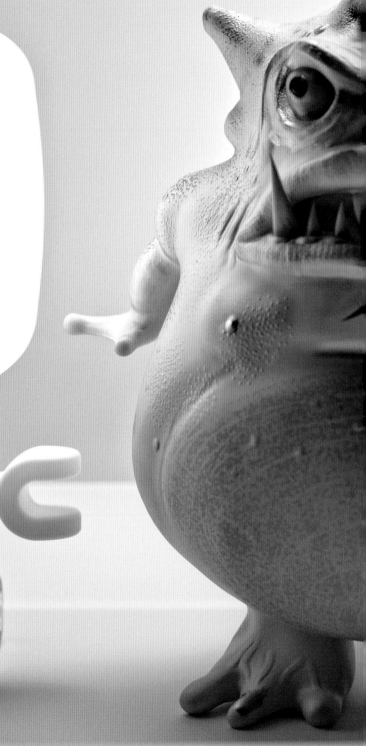

WE COME

The main focus of Büro für Form designstudio is on product, graphic, and lighting design and aceessoires for renowned, international clients.

The common thread running through the design is the well-balanced combination of organic shape and geometric elements, sometimes with a bit of humor, creating a particular modern style.

Mission statement:
"Products need more then perfect function and ergonomics, they need some poetry!"

SPACEBOT: Tablelamp & Stickergraphics for Belgian company DARK.be

ALIEN: Character & Animation for **LARGEMASSIVECOLLECTIVE**

© 2013 by Lars Korb, Constantin Wortmann

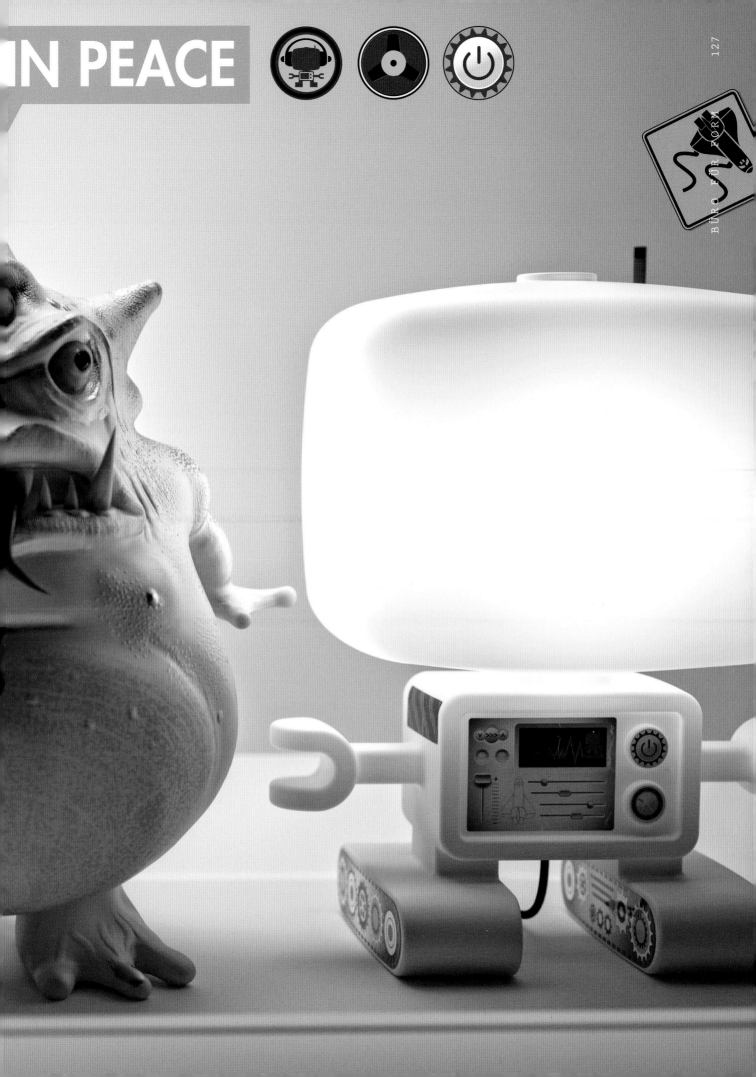

# Stroomberg

**Based in Amsterdam, The Netherlands, Philip Stroomberg (1967) is a graphic designer who works primarily in the cultural sector for clients including universities, publishers and art institutions. Stroomberg regularly creates designs that are used for the promotion of Dutch culture.**
**Stroomberg is always looking to turn content into shape, creating shapes based on content. An important feature of his work is interaction: his designs encourage the user to develop a bond with the object, and many of them challenge the users' imagination.**
www.stroomberg.net

**Beeldvenster** (2013)
'Beeldvenster' ('Picture Window') was designed to introduce a printing house's new identity. A portfolio of 13 photographs, it can be folded out into a free-standing triangular, pyramidal shape that is actually a picture frame for the display of the 13 images. The frame can be turned on its side, making it suitable for displaying both landscape and portrait format pictures.

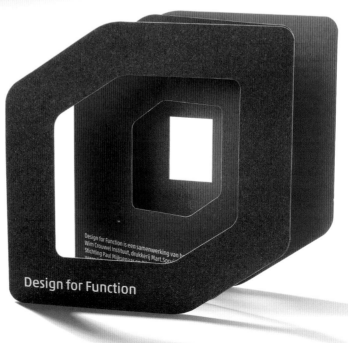

**Design for Function** (2013)
An invitation to the Design for Function ceremony, where two prizes were awarded: the Paul Mijksenaar Award for Functional Design, and the Mart.Spruijt Theatre Poster Award for best-designed theatre poster. The invitation is punched and folded in such a way that it transforms into a free-standing object.

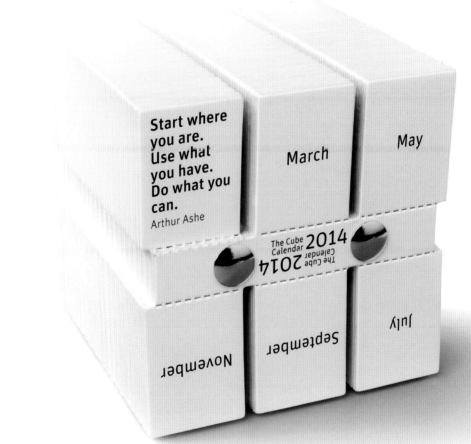

Start where
you are.
Use what
you have.
Do what you
can.
Arthur Ashe

March

May

The Cube
Calendar 2014

July

September

November

1
Wednesday
January

2014
starts
here

**The Cube Calendar** (2013)
The Cube Calendar adds an
innovative twist to the concept
of the tear-off calendar. Inspired
by thoughts about time, it is a
compact object that gradually
changes shape: by tearing off a
card each day, the user reveals
the workings of time.

# Freytag Anderson

Freytag Anderson is a Glasgow based design studio, launched in 2013 by Daniel Freytag and Greig Anderson. FA design for print, screen and the environment, working with clients that share their vision to communicate better with the world. Through an organic process of keen observation and bold thinking, they create design that represents true value and inspires greater connections. Ultimately they take brands from where they are, to where they want to be.

At the heart of all activities is a collaborative process. The success of their studio relies solely on the talented people they work with. Customised teams are built to reflect the needs of clients and the potential of the project. This hands-on creative thinking allows them to stay nimble and react in the most economic way to clients needs. Join in the conversation @FreytagAnderson or for more information visit www.freytaganderson.com

Left to Right:
_48 Miles Later, 2013 – Limited Edition Chilli Black Ale created for Fyne Ales and Brewdog Glasgow in collaboration with Matt Burns Design.
_The Fableists, 2013 – Identity for sustainable children's fashion label based in London.
_National Galleries Scotland, 2013 – Peter Doig: No Foreign Lands exhibition identity, signage and promotional materials.

The Trustees and Director-General of the National Galleries of Scotland invite you to the private view of:

**Peter Doig**
*No Foreign Lands*
**Friday 2 August 2013**
6.30–8.30pm

# DO

Scottish National Gallery
The Mound, Edinburgh
*Please enter via the Gardens Entrance*

Admits two
Entry by invitation only
*Please bring this invitation with you*

Please RSVP by Friday 26 July
Telephone 0131 624 6447 or email
development@nationalgalleries.org

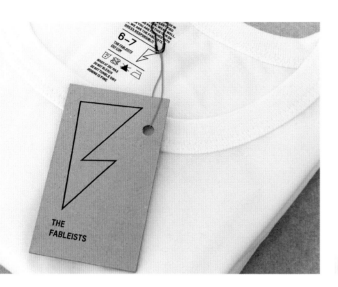

THE
FABLEISTS

SCOTTISH
NATIONAL
GALLERY

G

nds

eter Doig No Foreign Lands runs from 3 August
3 November 2013. The exhibition is organised
the National Galleries of Scotland and the
ontreal Museum of Fine Arts.

age: Pelican (Stag), 2003 (detail) © the artist.

Cricket Painting (Paragrand)
2006- 2012
Private Collection

SC
NA
GA

013

ffice
-mail

Peter Doig No Foreign L
to 3 November 2013. T
by the National Galleri
Montreal Museum of Fe

Image: Pelican (Stag), 2
National Galleries of Sc

## Room 6
*Figures II*

In his more recent figure paintings Doig has made
the human figure fit into a sharply delineated formal
structure – developing his interest of a few years
before in geometrical forms.

In *Paragon* and *Cricket Painting (Paragrand)* the
forms against which the cricketers are set are organic
and curvilinear - the blue tongues of the sea licking
the red beach, the green, hanging, fruit-like forms,
highlighted against the dark sky. In *House of Flowers
(See You There)* the central figure seems but a ghost
set against the geometrical patterns of the fence
and brick wall. A compromise between geometry
and nature is achieved in the two paintings of *Figure
by a Pool*. The three horizontal bands divided by
a distant sandy beach and a nearby diving board
are broken up into flat rectangles of colour· a
distant memory of American Abstract Expressionist

Imme & Alessio

WE WORK

FOR BIG COMPANIES

# we are Lion & BEE

♡ WE LOVE OUR JOB!

& SMALL FINE BUSINESS

BASED IN BERLIN WITH NO EMPLOYEES— JUST THE TWO OF US AND A LOT OF IDEAS.

WE LIKE TO SURPRISE YOU!

WE COMMUNICATE

# THIERRY POQUET

## TWEEDSTYLE

Thierry Poquet is a independent graphic
and stylist designer based in Aix en
provence, France. He works in his own
studio. He loves typography and the lost
art of handdrawN lettering and works
as designer and consultant of clothing
brands.

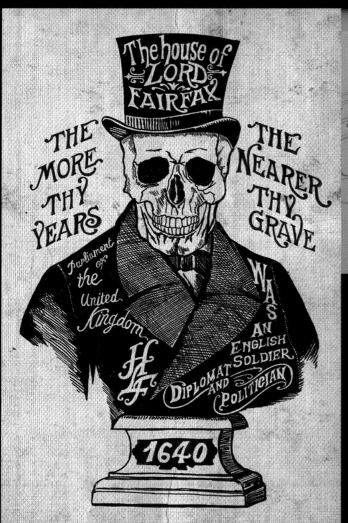

# JAMES MARTyN

James Martyn, 33, is a freelance graphic designer and photographer living and working in Portland, Oregon, USA. He creates unique and very personal identities, invitations, editorial pieces, and packages for fine people in the Pacific Northwest and beyond. Martyn's design aesthetic draws from the rise of the Rococo era and is sprinkled with typographic and design elements pulled from a variety of odds and ends found in antique shops throughout the Pacific Northwest. His designs are one of a kind and characterized by an acute attention to detail and the personality of every client that shines through each unique piece.

## HEXAPODA WINES / 2012

This 85th anniversary wine release needed to evoke the hard times these wine makers fell upon during prohibition, but it also needed to celebrate its survival and the enjoyment of its current success as the largest—still family owned and operated—winery in Colorado.

## APPLE'S AUTOMOTIVE / 2013

Though highly successful, Apple's Automotive never did have an identity. As a part-time farmer, Mervin, owner of the shop, did business with a firm handshake or a parts trade. That honesty and integrity comes through with an identity that is well-worn, yet timeless and still holding its own.

# OWEN DAVEY

Owen Davey was spotted at his degree show by Folio Illustration Agency when his career began and by demand alone is proving to be the man of the moment. His natural and extraordinary ability to capture just the right amount of heart and humour in his artwork epitomises the illustration industry worldwide. He works in a mixture of traditional and digital media creating insightful characters and scenes with a polished finish, honing in on feelings of nostalgia and future aspirations alike. His unique style combines a warm palette, muted colours, texture and pattern, which he playfully uses to engage a wide & varied audience. His illustrations and professional approach lend itself entirely to the realms of advertising, editorial and publishing across the board. Owen seems to be a master of all, producing extremely sophisticated animations in his studio, adding yet another string to his accomplished bow.

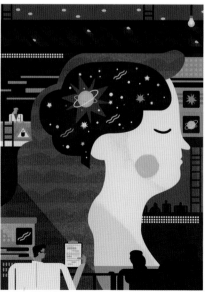

# BÜRO DESTRUCT

Title Font: «BD Pankow»
Design by Lopetz, 2013

Swiss Graphic Design Studio «Büro Destruct» founded in 1994 in Berne, currently includes the three members Lopetz (71), MBrunner (70) & H1reber (71). Since day one, BD has kept the boundary between art and commercial graphic design open, as testified to by the number and variety of techniques employed, and reflected in projects for clients from widely differing fields. Exhibitions, lectures and workshops around the world enable the Büro Destruct project continually evolve and to widen its contacts in Berne, the capital of Switzerland, in line with its motto:

«Small City – Big Design».

Character- and icon-designs
for Seabag Collection 2014.
Design by Lopetz, MBrunner
& H1reber, 2013.
Client: Kitchener AG, Bern

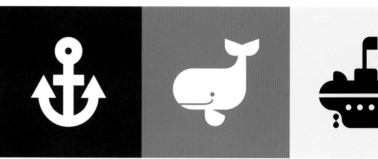

Clubnight invitation, «Stride» meets
«The Trilogy Tapes». Design by Lopetz, BD, 2013.
Client: Stridenight.com

Thursday October 17th 2013, Doors 22h
Rössli Bar Reitschule Bern
www.thetrilogytapes.com
www.stridenight.com

#8

STRIDE meets THE TRILOGY TAPES

ROSSLI BAR

STRIDE

Will Bankhead
(TTT)

Anthony Naples
(TTT, Mister Saturday Night,
Rubadub)

Madteo
(TTT, Hinge Finger, Sähkö,
Morphine, Workshop)

meet

Sassy J
(Stride, Patchwork)

Kev the Head
(Stride)

lopetz (büro destruct)

# SEVEN

Snowboard jacket design for the japanese brand «A-Seven»

Design by: Lopetz, 2013.
Art direction: Toshio Kondo & Akihiro Ikegoshi.
Photography: OKA-Z.
Client: Air to ground A-Seven (Descente Ltd).

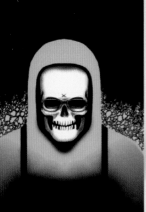

# POGO
## POWERED BY PIZZA™

POGO is an independent graphic artist, designer and hamburger lover from a beatiful and vibrant town called Mexico City. He specializes in graphic design and illustration, and spends most of his time doing branding, rock posters and personal art work. His many other secret talents include lettering, hand-drawing, bear taming, snake charming and clothing design. In addition, his work has been shown in different parts of the world and he has enchanted exotic land with his magnificient beard and pencil skills.

_LOGOS

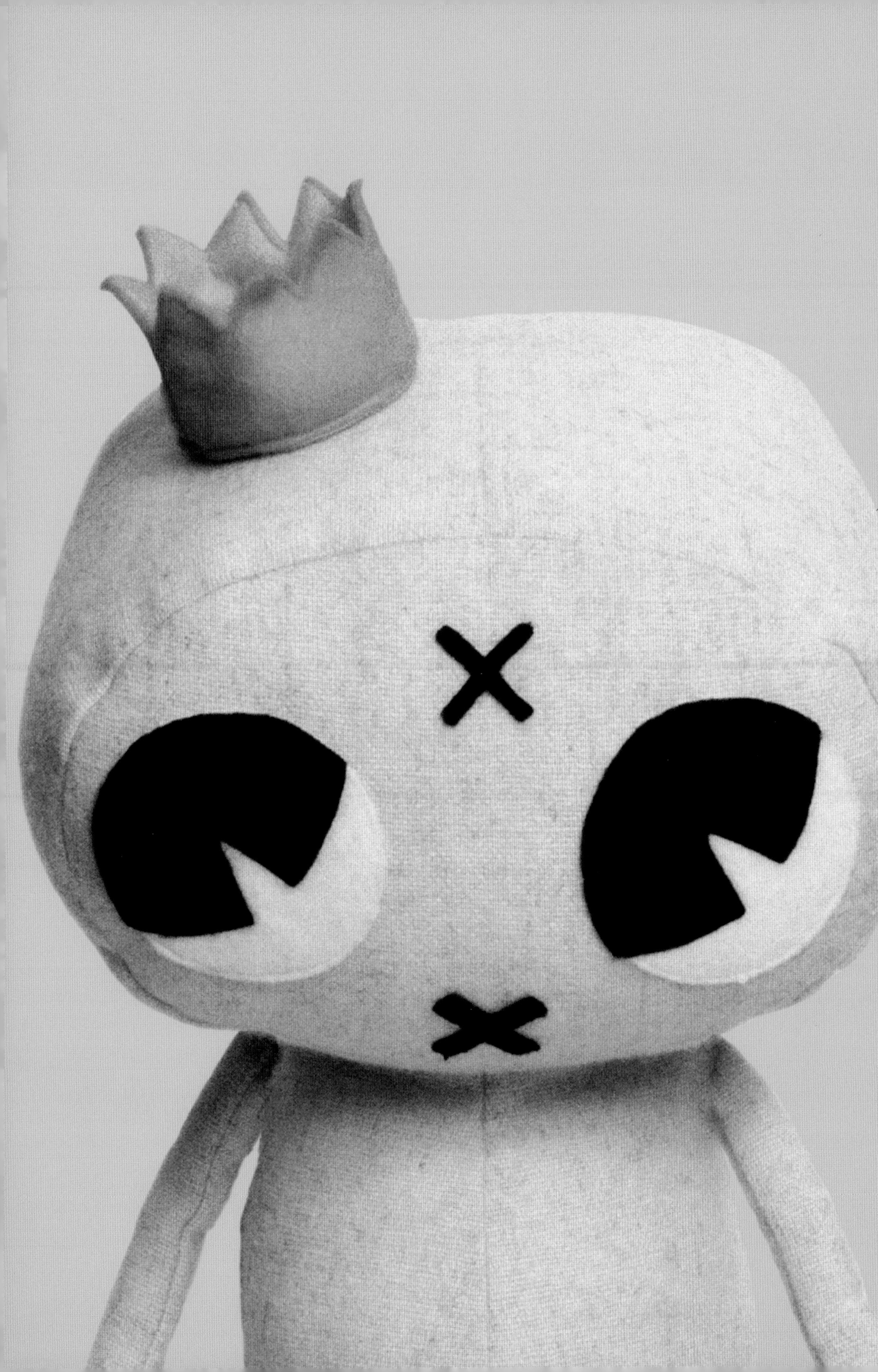

# Naroska

How do you visualize energy? How do you turn organic into luxury? How do you give Europe a profile? How to deal with stereotypes? Everything starts with a question — questioning facts; identifying a problem; getting to the heart of a matter; understanding something. These logos and signets have all been reduced to a question. The idea is the answer.
Marc Naroska was born 1969. Since 2000 he manages his Design Studio Naroska in Berlin.

Reiss-Engelhorn-Museen, Museums
Dublyooh, Consultancy
Christiane Weber & Company,
Gift service

Verein der Freunde und Förderer
des Mies van der Rohe Hauses,
Supporting association
C/O Berlin, Cultural institution
BigBlue, Bar

Berlin 775 years, Cultural event
E. Poetzsch Verlag, Scientific
publishing company
L144 - The Foundry, Heritage-
protected building
Popagenten, Music publishing
Exclusive Entertainment,
Event agency

Hype, Music publishing
Fresh Spirit, German
national sailing team
Stadtverwaltung Germering,
Logo of the community of
Germering
Wahrlich, Mineral oil
trading company
Mies van der Rohe Haus,
Anniversary logo

JM

MOO

VILLA
OPPENHEIM

SANTAVERDE

SINEMUS

High Tech Center Babelsberg,
Post production for visual
Media
Die Löffelei, Soup shop
JFM Consult, consultancy
Stadtverwaltung Potsdam,
Logo of the city of Potsdam
Sinemus, Fashion label

MeyerPartner, Accountants, lawyers
and management consulting
Hasso Plattner Ventures, Start-Up-
Incubator
M100 Sanssouci Colloquium, Annual
international Media Conference
smartmove, Service provider for the
energy industry
Kitepower, Kite surf school

One hundred years of German-Norwegian
encounters, Exhibition
Tchibo, Fashion line
Villa Oppenheim, Cultural landmark
Santaverde, Natural cosmetics company
Baltic Study Net, International
network of universities

Estepona Hills, Urbanization project
KEK - Koodinationsstelle für den
Erhalt des schriftlichen Kulturguts,
Coordination center
Villa Albatros, Apartments
Kiru, Shelfing systems
Cluster Labs, Berlin

# 344 Design

344 Design is the creative home of designer/ illustrator/writer **Stefan G. Bucher.** Born in 1973, Bucher is the man behind 344lovesyou.com and the popular online drawing and story-telling experiment dailymonster.com. He is the author of the books *100 Days of Monsters, All Access, The Graphic Eye, You Deserve a Medal—Honors on the Path to True Love, 344 Questions: The Creative Person's Do-It-Yourself Guide to Insight, Survival, and Artistic Fulfillment*, and *The Yeti Story,* which he wrote and illustrated exclusively for Saks Fifth Avenue. He has created designs for David Hockney, Judd Apatow, and The New York Times. D&AD honored him with a Yellow Pencil for book design, and the Art Directors Club of New York declared him a Young Gun. He designed the titles for the motion pictures "The Fall," "Immortals" and "Mirror, Mirror" by director Tarsem, and his time-lapse drawings appear on the Emmy-award winning TV show "The Electric Company."

The Blue Man Theater at the Monte Carlo Resort and Casino, Las Vegas, Nevada. Bucher was responsible for all aspects of the design, from the architecture of the main entrance portal and gift store to motion and window graphics, down to wall art and custom carpet design. Blue Man Group photographs by Emily Shur.

**Top:** The Saks Yeti. Bucher designed the Yeti character for luxury retailer Saks Fifth Avenue. Beyond developing the 14-inch plush character with Yottoy Inc., he provided the Yeti with an elaborate origin story, published in the book "The Yeti Story" by Harper Collins. **Bottom:** Main title for the movie "Mirror Mirror" by director Tarsem.

# KRONK

Studio Kronk is a semi-fictional studio based somewhere in South Africa and is dedicated to exploring passionate creative solutions for projects of all sizes, making beyond awesome products, and finding the perfect balance of logic, magic and coffee. This one-man-brand is the commercial home for graphic artist, Kris Hewitt, otherwise known as Kronk and has been known to enjoy collaborations with mercenary misfits from time to time who also possess skills that are, well... just not normal.

The studio strives to constantly have adventures of creativity with a conscience and find kickass ways to use graphic art and good ol' brainpower to push their work into new, fun and exciting realms.

**This page / Clockwise**
1 / "Saddest summer ever" Skateboard
2 / "Tail Grab" Skateboard
3 / "Tasty totem" Limited Ed. Surfboard,
Spur Steak Ranches Surf School
**Next page / Top Row / Left to Right**
1 / "Rat Basterd" Wristwatch
Vannen Watches / www.vannenwatches.com
Photo © Vannen Watches
2 / Wired Magazine Article Illustration
www.wired.com
Image © Condé Nast
3 / "Dweezil" Vinyl Figure
Kidrobot / www.kidrobot.com
Image © Kidrobot Inc.
**Middle Row /**
4 / "Tokolosh" Awareness Poster
Open Co Design / Campaign 4 Cancer
www.campaign4cancer.co.za
5 / "Killjoy" 20" Dunny Vinyl Figure
Kidrobot / www.kidrobot.com
6 / "Hip Hop" Poster Advertisment
Open Co Design / Muv-U
www.muv-u.co.za
**Bottom Row /**
7 / Kronk X Kidrobot Apparel Capsule Collection
Kidrobot / www.kidrobot.com
Image © Kidrobot Inc.
8 / "Brolly Girl" Limited Edition Print
Dutchmann Racing Poster Portfolio
www.dutchmann.co.za
9 / "Kidrobot" Mascot Logotype
Kidrobot / www.kidrobot.com
Image © Kidrobot Inc.
10 / Kronk x Butan "B5" Apparel Collaboration
Butan Wear / www.butanwear.com

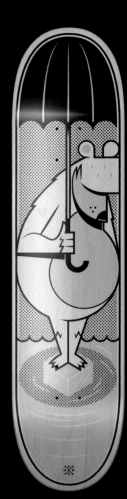

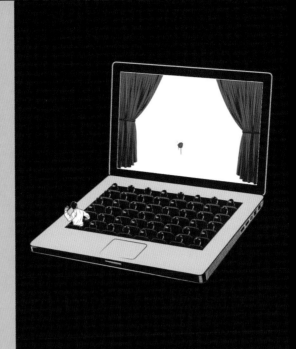

TEAM **DUTCHMANN**

KALAHARI SPEED WEEK ★ 14-23 SEPT '13

# Ghost

Ghost is a Norwegian multidisciplinary design studio specializing in visual identities, digital- and industrialdesign. The design studio was founded in 1998 and has 10 employees and 4 partners; Mats Henriksen (1972), Øyvind Krstian

Tendenes (1975), Paal Ariel Smith-Hofstad (1980), Runar Lillegård (1982). We use design as a strategic process for creating strong brands, good products and great customer experiences

1.

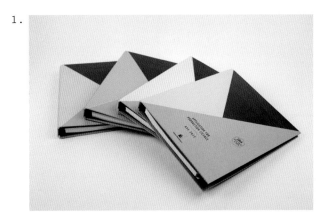 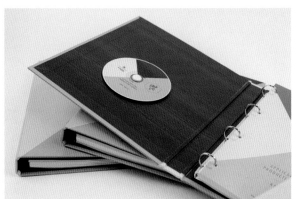

2.

1.Visual indentity for an application for production licence for Faroe Petroleum.
2.Visual identity for Org Geophysical.
3.Packaging for a pedagogical childrens' puzzle.

3.

1.

# Designers United

2.

Designers United is a multidisciplinary design agency focused in brand identity development, creative direction, and interaction based in Thessaloniki, Greece. It was brought into being in 2005 when Dimitris Koliadimas and Dimitris Papazoglou decided to join forces and engage visual research and systematic methodology into the design process. The company has been creating integrated design solutions for a diverse range of international clients across various industries, scales and budgets. Their extensive experience and dedication is reflected in their portfolio – now spanning for more than eight years of vibrant, fresh and engaging visual communication.

3.

**1. European Design Awards 2012 Catalogue.** Art direction and design for the 2012 European Design Awards catalogue, featuring the Jury-selected best that the European communication design industry has to offer.

**2. Beauty of Speed.** The Volvo V60 T5 was transformed into an artwork in order to raise public awareness in Greece for Volvo Ocean Race 2011-2012, the world's greatest sailing adventure. The abstract form of the water splash becomes the significant element of the graphic environment, representing the dynamics of all elements involved in the race (water, wind, weather conditions) and implying the notion of human interaction with technology and nature for a greater cause.

**3. 5 Olive Oil.** Brand identity and packaging design for a new premium quality series of Greek extra virgin olive oil. 5 stands for quintessence in olive oil.

# Brogen Averill

Brogen Averill Studio's portfolio comprises major assignments for a "who's who" of international brands as well as an enviable selection of niche design projects. Working with some of the world's most successful companies and individuals, we have gained an international reputation, producing versatile and innovative design. Returning from Europe to New Zealand in 2004, Brogen Averill

Match Exhibition:

Showcasing works by 8 photographers.

RWNU 200074 4
22G1

MAX. GROSS    30.480 KG
              67.200 LBS

TARE          2.220 KG
              4.890 LBS

NET           28.260 KG
              62.310 LBS

CU. CAP.      33.2 CU.M.
              1.170 CU.FT.

# Studio

Studio was established.
We create: brand and identity development, packaging, print, editorial, signage, wayfinding systems and website design and development. We create concept lead design,

Poster.

investigating requirements and translating them into solutions that are intelligent, creatively inspiring and ultimately different. Design - in all its forms - continues to drive our creative ethos.

brogenaverill.com

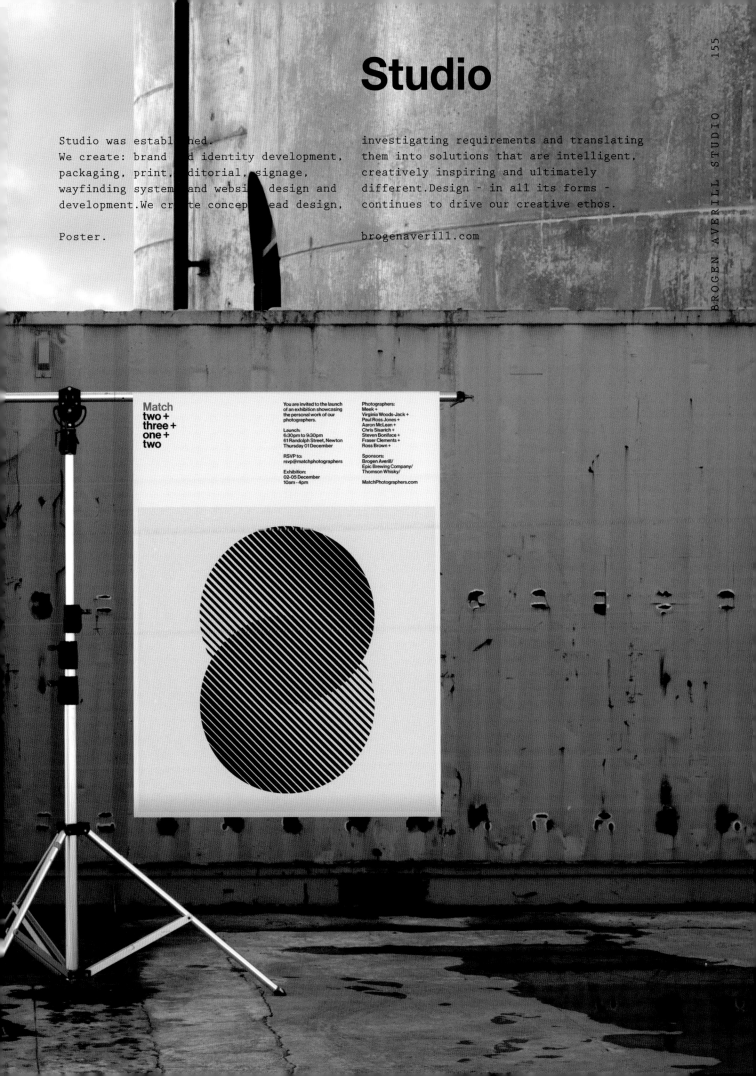

Match
two +
three +
one +
two

You are invited to the launch of an exhibition showcasing the personal work of our photographers.

Launch:
6:30pm to 9:30pm
61 Randolph Street, Newton
Thursday 01 December

RSVP to:
rsvp@matchphotographers

Exhibition:
02-05 December
10am - 4pm

Photographers:
Meek +
Virginia Woods-Jack +
Paul Ross Jones +
Aaron McLean +
Chris Sisarich +
Steven Boniface +
Fraser Clements +
Ross Brown +

Sponsors:
Brogen Averill/
Epic Brewing Company/
Thomson Whisky/

MatchPhotographers.com

# Andrew Gorkovenko

Andrew Gorkovenko is an advertising designer who specializes in branding and is based in Moscow. He mainly works on corporate and product identity development, package design, printwork – such as annual reports for companies like Allianz – broschures, calanders. He is also involved in web design and illustration.

Macaroni «Pasta La Vista».

This project involved the development of trademark and packaging for Pasta La Vista macaroni products. Pasta La Vista  is a brand which produces a wide range of hand-made macaroni products manufactured in accordance with traditional Italian recipes and ingredients of only the highest quality.

«TripTea» tea.

At the heart of brand communication is the idea of traveling to exotic countries of the world. The packaging is decorated with landscapes from the countries where it was assembled and produced. All landscapes are handmade directly from the tea variety in the package. This conveys an exotic image of the country as well as the richness of flavors and nuances of the product itself.

# Marta Cerdà

Marta Cerdà (1980) is a Graphic Designer, Illustrator and letterer currently based in Barcelona. At the end of 2008, she won the Art Director's Club Young Guns 6th edition and opened with her own studio. Since then she has worked on projects that require art direction, design, illustration and custom typography for arts, culture and advertising clients.

SPAIN
arts &
culture

2012
SPANISH CULTURAL
PROGRAM
Fall | Winter

Spain Arts and Culture, 2012. Magazine cover illustration

Atoms for Peace, 2013. Lettering self-project

François Chalet has been working as an independant illustrator, animator, director and visual artist for national and international clients in the cultural and commercial sectors since 1997.

His clients include eBay Europe, the Swiss national exhibition Expo 02, the Centre Georges Pompidou, Mitsubishi Japan, MTV Europe Music Awards, Nuit Blanche Paris, Philippe Starck, Prima Linea Productions France and the company Thomas Duchatelet.

Chalet has taught at various universities at home and abroad and was professor and head of programmes for the studies Motiondesign in Berlin at the Berlin Technical Art College from 2007-2008. From 2008 to 2012 he tought animation at the Zurich University of the Arts (ZHdK) in the study course of Cast (audiovisual Media) and since 2012 heads the Animation Studies of Lucerne University of Arts & Design.

www.francoischalet.ch

# François Chalet

right: Book projekt (Echtzeit Verlag, CH), 2014, daily illustrations / topic: father and son

center: Miss Ko (Restaurant, Paris, FRA, designed by Philippe Starck), 2013, animated Dragon for the screentables

left: Demain j'ai rencontré (FRA) / A demain (JAP), 2011, visual Art for two pieces of the french contemporary dance company Thomas Duchatelet

# Morphoria Design Collective

Morphoria Design Collective is a colla-boration of seven designers based in Düsseldorf, Berlin and Stuttgart. Looking for the right framework for their way of thinking and working to-gether, the collective was founded to combine all the different speciali-zations of its members, ranging from editorial design to exhibition design to corporate design. This interaction of different skills and interests is reflected in client work as well as in self-initiated projects like the Deaf Magazine.

www.morphoria.com

DEAF MAGAZINE: A multimedia magazine for and about the culture of German sign language, connecting printed and digital information via an augmented reality system (on mobile devices).

REINTRODUCE: A documentation about the work of former students of Prof. Uwe J.
Reinhardt and their way of thinking about design. In cooperation with Lisa Jacob.

DIE GROSSE: Visual identity and exhibition design for "DIE GROSSE Kunstausstellung
NRW 2013" in Düsseldorf, Germany.

# Mirko Ilić Corp.

Mirko Ilić Corp. is a New York-based studio specializing in graphic design, illustrations, and 3D animation, with a wide range of work from cultural manifestations to editorial design to high luxury hotels and restaurants.

"O." is the symbol for Oktobarski Art Salon. It was created with a positive and negative space and used as a frame for photography. That year's theme was repetition and order.

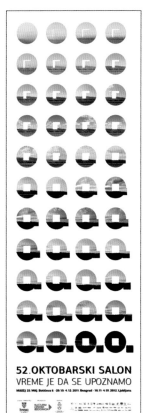

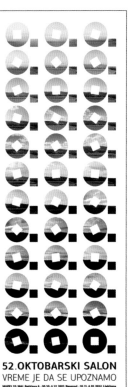

6th annual Jewish Film Festival was themed Tolerance. For the logo, part of the Star of David was transformed into a heart, a symbol for love and tolerance. 7th JFF had the theme of Equality. The Star of David was created out of three different colored equal signs.

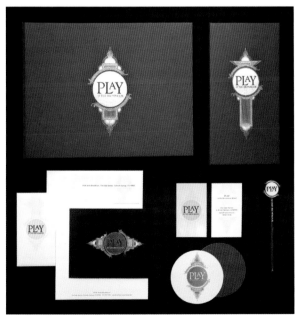

The identity for this restaurant was inspired by the American gaslight style from the late 1800s because The Broadmoor Hotel in Colorado Springs was established in 1891. The logo's decorative elements surround a circle alluding to the bowling alley inside the restaurant.

Original Motion Picture Score
Music Composed by Gato Barbieri

ERTO GRIMALDI Production
Marlon Brando

A Japanese super sonic group designs music and musics design. Works take on multiple forms such as recordings, visual installation, writing, application, cross stitch, and live performance. In 2001, exhibition and performance at P.S.1/MoMA, New York. Solo expo at RAS gallery, Barcelona, 2004. "D-Day design today," 2005, Centre Georges Pompidou, Paris.
2004 publication of "Designin' in the rain" (ACTAR, Barcelona.) Nine music albums released - so far. Founded "Re<ords," a record label, iPhone/iPad Appli, 2009. Founded "b00g," an electronic book label, iPhone/iPad Appli, 2010. New projects, sound: "Dave, I See" (muzak), vision: "Crumple, Don't Record" (ceramic art).
They call themselves "Artoonist" (Artoon means art + cartoon.)
And "Say it low, we are human being and we're proud."
http://www.delaware.gr.jp/

# Delaware

Project: Crumple, Don't Record.
Left: Last Tango In Paris
Right: Lou Reed
Year: 2013

Lou Reed
Rock And Roll Diary
1967–1980

Project: Crumple, Don't Record.
Left: Last Tango In Paris
Right: Lou Reed
Year: 2013

# Elroy Klee

Former graffiti artist and owner of a
design studio with 12 people,
ELROY KLEE, is a freelance art director
/ illustrator working in fields of
concepting, illustration, 3D and set
design. His work is a mixture of urban
street art, experimental transformer
style, typo and a bit of Dutch design
with extraordinairy use of color and
craftmanship.

If you want to see more then check
www.elroyklee.com

Elroy Klee
Art direction & Brand design
Enschede, Holland
Follow on Twitter    @elroyklee
Like on Facebook     elroykleepage

Untitled set design 1

# Osh Grassi

Osh Grassi is a 27-years-old graphic designer & photographer born in Buenos Aires, Argentina. She currently lives at San Isidro city, by the riverside, a very beautiful and inspiring place. She studied Graphic Design at the University of Buenos Aires and graduated in the year 2009. After a tour around Europe;

collecting inspiration and good stories; Osh is now a freelance designer who works for the most important advertising agencies and studios around the globe.

As a hobby she teaches photography at Motivarte! Photography School.

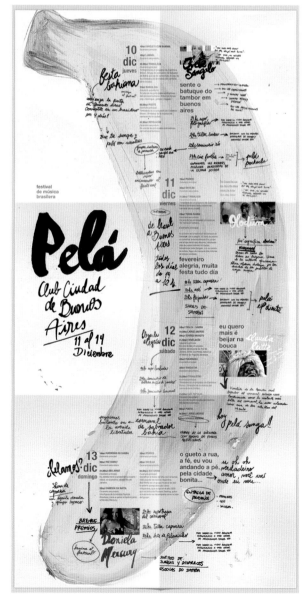

Pelá - Brazilian Festival (2009) is a graduation project made for the University of Buenos Aires. Both the event and venue are fictitious.

Pelá is a festival about Brazil and it's culture. The naming came from the spanish verb for "peel" (pelá) which also means "to take out", so the concept is to take your clothes off and feel like a Brazilian on carnival.

festival
de música
brasilera

Pelá

Club Ciudad
de Buenos
Aires
11 al 14
Diciembre

# HLYNUR INGÓLFSSON

Hlynur Ingólfsson is a graphic designer from Reykjavik Iceland, born in 1984.
He studied at the Iceland Academy of the Arts from 2009-2012 and has been working in the field of graphic design ever since, mostly for an international television show and also some freelance work on the side.

The Gelato typeface was created in a typography course at the Iceland Academy of the Arts in 2011. It was originally created as a childish, silly type so the name gelato and the pastel colors reflect on the whole purpose of the typeface.
www.hlynuringolfsson.com

THE QUICK BROWN MR. FOX
JUMPS OVER THE
LAZY DOGG

AÁBCÐDEÉFGHIÍ

JKLMNOÓPQRST

UÚVWXYÝZÞÆÖ

(1234567890)

?!!#%./

._.:.-._

**A Trip to India**, Brazil 2012.
This is a self-published book, containing many illustrations (some shown on the opposite page) specially designed for this edition. These patterns were inspired by the photographs shown in the book.

## VISITA A MAHABALIPURAM

O programa daquela manhã era conhecer esse conjunto de monumentos históricos, composto por construções magníficas e diversas esculturas, também conhecido como Mallahapuram.

O primeiro monumento, chamado *A Penitência de Arjuna*, retrata cenas do *Mahabharata* em que estão esculpidas elefantes, macacos, leões, apsaras (deusas dançarinas) e outras figuras mitológicas, com destaque especial para Shiva e Arjuna, o grande guerreiro homenageado. Quando a guia percebeu que eu já tinha ouvido falar daqueles personagens, passou a me olhar com outros olhos, e eu, boba, fiquei toda prosa com meus parcos conhecimentos do vasto poema.

Este monumento, em termos de detalhes na pedra esculpida, é lindíssimo e muito sofisticado. Porém fica colado na beira da rua, com pouca perspectiva para ser apreciado. Para atrapalhar mais ainda, havia um enxame de vendedores ambulantes oferecendo, insistentemente, pequenas esculturas, livretos, cartões-postais e sei lá o que mais. Aliás, como em qualquer ponto turístico, em qualquer lugar do mundo.

A *Penitência de Arjuna*, RETRATA CENAS DO MAHABHARATA EM QUE ESTÃO ESCULPIDAS ELEFANTES, MACACOS, LEÕES, APSARAS (DEUSAS DANÇARINAS) E OUTRAS FIGURAS MITOLÓGICAS.

O *Taj Mahal*, EM TODO SEU ESPLENDOR. EU IMAGINAVA ALGO GRANDIOSO, MAS BEM A ELEGÂNCIA E O REFINAMENTO ESTÉTICO QUE ENCONTREI.

Nesses momentos, um bom guia compensa as chatices ocasionais da falação em excesso, explicações históricas etc. Felizmente, nossos guias foram excelentes. E quando um deles começou a querer mostrar serviço demais, foi logo dispensado.

Outro elemento usado na requintada ornamentação das paredes do Taj que me deixou boquiaberta foram as telas esculpidas, como uma renda, em uma única placa de mármore. Também fiquei fascinada com os desenhos florais. Consegui identificar tulipas, íris e papoulas entre as

# ⊂ᴅ Celina Carvalho DESIGN

Born in 1975, Celina Carvalho has more than fifteen years of experience designing for publishing companies and design studios. Celina holds an MFA in Design from the School of Visual Arts, in New York, and a BA in Visual Communication, from PUC University in Rio de Janeiro. Celina worked as a designer and art director, at Abrams Books in New

York, for five years. Prior to that, she was a designer and art editor for four years at *Editora Abril*. Based in Rio de Janeiro, Brazil, since 2007, Celina Carvalho Design has developed work for a variety of clients and licensors, including Rizzoli International, *Editora Record*, *Editora Rocco*, Vogue, Fox, CBS, and DC Comics, among others.

swedish post office

school of visual arts

rosenworld is a design, illustration and animation studio.
actually there is no studio, rosenwald works alone, and
rosenworld doesn't exist. in spite of this,
www.rosenworld.com was launched in 1995. she authored
"all the wrong people have self-esteem", an inappropriate
book for young ladies, and frankly, anybody else. david
sedaris and rosenwald have collaborated on "david's
diary", an animated app. laurie teaches an incredibly
popular workshop called "how to make mistakes on
purpose" and appeared as "woman" on "the sopranos",
a role she was born to play.

politically incorrect interview:
http://yourdreamsmynightmares.com/post/4101119502
7/your-dreams-my-nightmaresepisode-041-an

animation:

https://vimeo.com/58140674

https://vimeo.com/27496792

https://vimeo.com/17057593

american illustration

the new york times

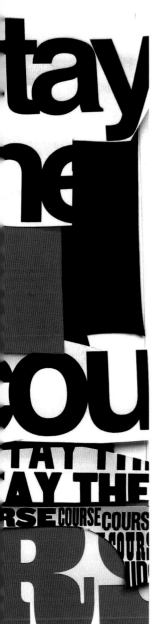

ker

target stores billboards in times square

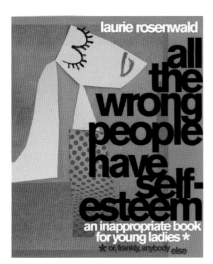

bloomsbury

# HAYES

Carlos Hayes Abreu, was born in Lisbon, Portugal. He´s a Graphic Designer/illustrator currently working as Creative Director at Lisbon based Ad agency Sumo. As an artist he collaborated with brands like Mtv and WeSC, for the first limited edition WeSC headphones ever made in Portugal. He also worked for clients such as adidas, Yamaha, Piaggio and American Express.

WeSC by Hayes
Limited Edition headphones.
2010

"Timeless is not Forever" Poster Series. 2012

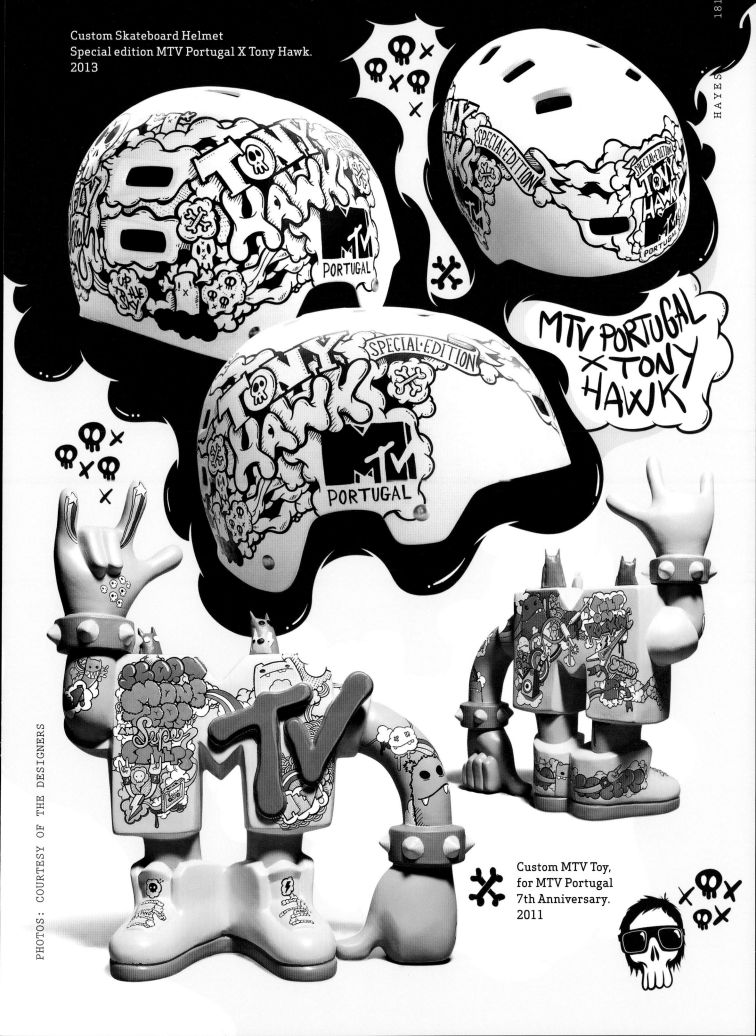

Custom Skateboard Helmet
Special edition MTV Portugal X Tony Hawk.
2013

MTV PORTUGAL X TONY HAWK

Custom MTV Toy,
for MTV Portugal
7th Anniversary.
2011

# STEVE SIMPSON

Steve Simpson is an award winning freelance illustrative designer based in Ireland with over 30 years experience in the industry. Steve's traditional approach allows him to combine both illustration and design seamlessly through his use of limited colour palettes and hand drawn typography creating unified eye-catching designs that have earned him global acclaim. Steve starts every project with pencil and paper exploring multiple design directions for each job. Once pencils are approved he'll only then start the digital process of colouring, usually in Photoshop.

SMORGASBOARD is a board game for foodies created in Ireland. Players take on the guise of aspiring chefs as they work their way around the board in search of gastronomic success. The object of the game is to be the first team of chefs to graduate from Rick's Culinary Academy! The loser... does the dishes!

STEVE SIMPSON

The brief for the CHILLY MOO frozen yogurt range was to create an eye-catching design that would instantly appeal to kids and get the 'healthy' message across to parents.

Founding father of the Arts & Crafts Movement, WILLIAM MORRIS, once said *"Why run a newspaper ad featuring nothing but words? How about putting flowers on that tissue box? Wouldn't it be great if everything from magazines and brochures to food packages and road signs looked terrific while offering information?"* ...and yes, even barcodes!

MIC'S CHILLI has quickly grown from a start-up only a few years ago to a highly successful award winning enterprise exporting from Ireland to fine food emporiums across Europe. MicsChilli.ie

# MARTIN GREGUS

graphic design\photography

**WEAR THE NEWS™ \ ART CALENDAR \ 2013**
THIS 100cm x 65cm, 12 months, 13-page art calendar is the first of the Biggest Calendars Collection. Custom-made fine arts prints, hand-bound into an unique collectors edition. Art direction, photography and design by Martin Gregus, Wear the News handmade paper gowns by Elena Gregusova, Model: Barbara Gregusova, Made by PhotoFabrica™

**ONE 50 CANADA SOCIETY \ CORPORATE IDENTITY \ 2013**
Corporate name and identity for a not for profit society dedicated to supporting, planing, and executing projects related to the 150 years of Canada celebration in 2017.

• Martin Gregus MFA
• Vancouver\Bratislava\Salzburg

Graphic designer, photographer and visual artist Martin Gregus works in the fields of commercial, document, fine art and fashion photography. In graphic design Martin's main focus is on producing complete corporate identity solutions, website design, book and magazine design, illustration and computer art.
Over the last 25 years Martin worked around the world for agencies like BBDO, DDB, Grey or Young & Rubicam and many international renowned customers such as SAP, McDonald's, Levi's, UPS, IBM, Ford, Mercedes Benz, One 50 Canada Society. In the meantime Martin has been working together with his son Martin Jr. on publishing and exhibitions projects.
martin@martingregus.com

# LORENZO P

WAS BORN IN

AFTER STUDYING GRAPHIC ARTS IN MILAN, HE MO

AFTER HIS RE
HE WENT O
WITH SOI
GREA
COMMUI
AGEI

HE THEN TOOK SOME DISTANCE FROM THE ADVERTISING WORLD I

HIS·PASSION·FOI
AND·HIS·F

FOR·THE·19TH·CENT

ILLUSTF

*He uses images from te
dating back to that period which he*

★★★★★★ HIS ARE PROFOUNDLY UNIQUE ◎
ILLUSTRATIONS, WHICH GIVE LIFE BACK
★★ TO WORDS, EVENTS AND CHARACTERS
THAT WOULD OTHERWISE BE FORGOTTEN.
HE HAS USED HIS ART TO

*He now lives in Milan, he is a member of th*

AND HE POSITIVEI

TRANTONI

ENOA IN 1970.

TO FRANCE TO WORK AS A PRESS ART DIRECTOR.

URN TO ITALY,

TO WORK

E OF THE

TEST

CATION

CIES.

DER TO FULLY DEDICATE HIS TIME TO HIS ILLUSTRATING CAREER.

GRAPHIC DESIGN

SCINATION

RY COMBINE IN HIS

ATIONS

books and dictionaries

covered while browsing booksellers.

CREATE CAMPAIGNS FOR PRESTIGIOUS BRANDS, HE HAS WORKED WITH ★★★★ INTERNATIONAL MAGAZINES AND HE HAS HAD EXHIBITIONS IN MANY SHOWS ALL AROUND THE WORLD.

9ème Demi Brigade de Ligne in Marengo

Y LOVES PERRIER.

# Good Karma Creative

After graphic designer George Lois
retired from his 40 year ad agency career as
an owner and creative director,
he and his son Luke, a photographer and
digital design whiz, formed
Good Karma Creative in Manhattan.
Besides branding and creating
ad campaigns, they have written, designed
and produced numerous books
on graphic design.

## TRAVALO (2012- )

The refillable, aircraft-approved perfume container
with a patented, leak-proof filling system.
Simply pump and fill from your favorite fragrance
spray bottle, and you're ready to go.

Never
*Travalo*
without
them.

Travalo, the refillable perfume container, is the most awarded new beauty product in the last decade.
(Elle magazine called Travalo, "The most genius beauty gadget, ever!"). Women worldwide keep it handy, even when they go out shopping,
or for a quick spritz or two at the office – and Travalo's are aircraft-approved to take in your
carry-on luggage, all over the world! No assembly, no spills, no kidding – available in spray or rollerball in over a dozen classic styles.
Merely refill directly from your favorite fragrance bottle, in seconds, with no possibility of any spills!
And never Travalo without it.

(Our brilliant refill mechanism is patented, so beware of purchasing a cheap knock-off that leaks.)
Available at travalo.com or at most health and beauty stores worldwide.

## SUPERFOCUS (2010- )

By moving a tiny slider on the bridge of
revolutionary Superfocus glasses, you can focus
on the page of a book, a computer screen,
a movie, or a distant mountain.
Custom-made to your prescription, now you
can see the world...in Superfocus!
Originally named Trufocals, our new Superfocus
brand name instantly helped make
these brilliantly engineered glasses an
eye-popping marketing success.

SEE THE WORLD, FAR AND NEAR, IN SUPERFOCUS!

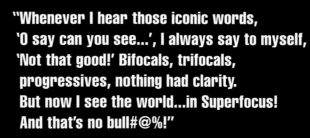

# Christina Föllmer

PHOTOS: COURTESY OF THE DESIGNER
* in collaboration with Catrin Sonnabend

CONZEPTS +
POSTERS

CATALOGUE +
BROCHURES

BOOKS +
MAGAZINES

LOGOS

FONTS

These three words are from a quote by Mark Twain which is one of the most inspiring for me personally and for my work. The quote itself describes an attitude towards life, but these words describe exactly what the creative process is about. DREAM stands for imagination, perception, creating and fantazising. EXPLORE for questioning, experimenting and researching, and DISCOVER describes inventing, developing, finding solutions and visualizing. In other words, I always try to let personality and character, knowledge and information, skills and competence play central roles in my work. Of course, the results are always customized to the (clients) briefing, the task or the project.  www.christinafoellmer.de

www.zolotogroup.ru

# ZOLOTOgroup

Moscow Agency ZOLOTOgroup is a union of marketing specialists and graphic designers. It is a creative lab for unique Russian brands, advertising communication and navigation of public spaces and facilities.

Brand is not merely a logo, but rather a system of ideas and values, which are embedded in the company's philosophy. According to ZOLOTOgroup specialists, dynamic branding is the most efficient way of interaction with the consumer, which we view as an underlying trend to replace frozen logo, and which allows us to quickly and easily explore spaces and increase awareness and loyalty among consumers. In this approach practically everything becomes the tool for brand communication — navigation of public space, promotional merchandise, staff uniform etc.

MOSCOW

Krimskaya Embankment / Identity / 2013

The Danilovskaya Manufacture
/ Signage / 2013

The All-Russian Exhibition / Identity / 2013

The ZIL Culture Centre/ Identity / 2012

**КУЛЬТУРНЫЙ
центр**

# VALLÉE DUHAMEL

Vallée Duhamel is a studio founded by Julien Vallée and Eve Duhamel. The studio creates images and videos for a wide range of clients from events to commercials, music, fashion, posters, magazines and objects. Vallée Duhamel specializes in high quality, lo-fi, and often handmade visuals and installations, and favours a playful and experimental approach toward work.

### REASONS TO BE CREATIVE
Main titles for the Brighton, UK Festival. The titles presents all the speakers from the event.

## SMASH PONG!

Ping Pong is an installation made for the exhibition On! Handcrafted Digital Playground, curated by Héctor Ayuso and exhibited at the Contemporary Art Center of Cincinnati.

## MISTEUR VALAIRE

Cover art and album design for the album Bellevue, from Montreal electro-jazz band Misteur Valaire.

The cover and a lot of the images were shot on location in the cold winter of Quebec's countryside.

# Tom Schamp illustrator

Tom is a Belgian illustrator with a unique, colorful style that appeals to both adults and children alike. He grew up - and still lives - close to the European capital (Brussels) yet his artistic influences come from all around the globe. Tom creates hand-painted images for a broad mix of international customers and his assignments cover a large range of media including books and magazine covers, publicity campaigns, posters, postcards, stamps, websites, calendars, packaging design, toys, children's furniture and even bicycles. His picture books, of which about 30 were published over the last10 years, have been translated into multiple languages. Most recently, his Otto-series was translated into complex Chinese (Maitian, 2013) and English (Tate Publishing, 2013).

much more to see on **www.tomschamp.com**          (& also on **www.facebook.com/TomSchampIllustrator**)

the summer of '76
tv guide cover illustration (VPRO 2012 Holland)

# IAN WHITEMAN AAdip

Ian Whiteman graduated from the Architectural Association in London in 1970 but has worked independently most of his professional life in the areas of book design, typography and the allied fields of logo design, branding and general graphics with an emphasis on classic English typography and Arabic Islamic design and calligraphy.

He has a lengthy client list, principally in the USA and the UK but also in South Africa, the Carribean, Spain and Central Europe. He was born in May 1945 near Cambridge UK, but now lives in Andalusia, Spain. He is married with four children and six grandchildren who are a mixture of German, English, American and Spanish parents. He has always had an involvement with music, both professionally and otherwise which can can be accessed on his web site.

**www.ianwhiteman.com**
**email: cwdm.typography@gmail.com**

o

**SAMPLE PAGES FROM A 2013 PROJECT FOR** ZAYTUNA COLLEGE, BERKELEY. CALIFORNIA. 68pp CATALOGUE. DESIGN, TYPESETTING. LOGOTYPE.

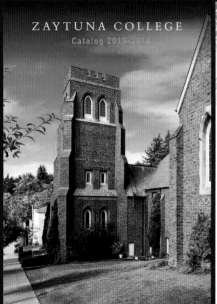

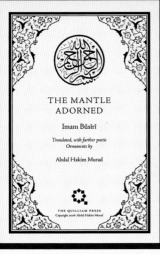

SAMPLE PAGES FROM THE
BOOK THE MANTLE ADORNED
2009 FOR QUIILIAM PRESS,
CAMBRIDGE, UK.

ENGLISH TYPESETTING OF
ORIGINAL TURKISH
PRODUCTION.

IAN WHITEMAN

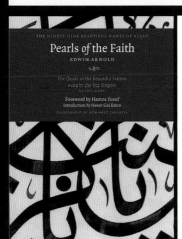

SAMPLE PAGES FROM THE
BOOK PEARLS OF THE FAITH 2006
FOR SANDALA INC. SAN FRANCSCO

PAGE DESIGN, TYPOGRAPHY, COVER
+ LOGOTYPE

SCOTT FISK

Scott Fisk is a Professor of Graphic Design at Samford University in Birmingham, AL, USA. Scott stays busy teaching and running "Scott Fisk Creative," a design firm specializing in branding and web design. He graduated first in his class from Memphis College of Art with an MFA in Computer Art and received his BFA in Graphic Design from Henderson State University. Scott's interests include web design, typography, photography, motion graphics and multimedia. He began his career in graphic design in 1994 at NetM Communications, an interactive agency with customers in the US, Canada, Australia, and the Europe. Since then, Scott has lived and worked

in the United States and Britain. Scott's work is part of permanent collections in numerous galleries and museums including the US National Archives. Scott is an active member of the American Institute of Graphic Arts (AIGA) and serves as a Birmingham AIGA board member and Educational Chair. Scott enjoys traveling with his wife Timarie who shares his peculiar interest in broadsides, ephemera, and antique printing processes. You can visit Scott's website at www.scottfisk.com.

THIS LETTERPRESS POSTER HAS BEEN SHOWN IN MUSEUMS AND GALLERIES AROUND THE WORLD AS PART OF THE HAITI POSTER PROJECT. EACH POSTER IS SOLD FOR $50 AND ALL PROCEEDS ARE GOING TO HELP THOSE IN NEED IN HAITI.

POSTER SHOWN IN VARIOUS SHOWS TO BRING ATTENTION TO THE WATER SCARCITY AND SANITATION CRISES AROUND THE WORLD.

THIS POSTER WAS DESIGNED FOR THE UNIVERSITY OF ALABAMA BIRMINGHAM'S WRITERS' SERIES.

*jeh.it*

Milano_Italy

jekyll & hyde is an italian graphic design
and communication studio founded in 1996
by marco molteni and margherita monguzzi.
the studio approach to design is based on close
cooperation with clients, coordinated target-oriented
planning and connection of all visual languages
and media.
jekyll & hyde designs for italian and multinational
companies and institutions, ranging from technology
to music and contemporary art.

closes-up of different projects made for:
ev4 *fashion brand* 2009, mogg unlimited design
*furniture manufacturer* 2012, must *lifestyle magazine*
2009, SPD Scuola Politecnica di Design
*educational institution*.2012

# jekyll & hyde

# JAUME OSMAN GRANDA

Jaume Osman Granda is a designer from Vilanova i la Geltrú, near Barcelona. He studied multimedia programming at the Polytechnic University in Terrassa. He first worked designing web pages and was later hired by Gominola as a flash programmer.

After a couple of years, tired of action script, he moved onto motion and started working for the Multipase studio, specialized in designing visuals for dance clubs. After some time, he started to work for the Barcelona-based studio Pornographics, where he spent two more years doing a little bit of everything, until he got tired of Barcelona and went back to his home town to work from home, where he keeps on taking part in all kinds of projects as a freelance.

WWW.JAUMEOSMAN.COM / WWW.OSMANGRANDA.COM

## NAME
# EDUARDO BERTONE

STARTED HIS CAREER IN THE LATE '90S IN
ARGENTINA. SOON AFTER, HE GOT INVOLVED
IN NUMEROUS INTERNATIONAL PROJECTS. HIS
OWN PARTICULAR WAY OF UNDERSTAND THE
WORLD, AND HIS PASSION FOR ART BROUGHT
HIM TO SHOW HIS WORK IN DIFFERENT PARTS
OF THE WORLD, TAKING PART IN EXHIBITIONS
AND IN COUNTLESS PUBLICATIONS IN BOOKS
AND MAGAZINES. ✗
NOW HE IS BASED IN MADRID, SPAIN.

## BEAR FLAG WINES®

— LABELS ARTWORK SERIES FOR RED AND
WHITE TABLE WINE. CALIFORNIA, USA.

2010 - 2012
Year

EDUARDO BERTONE

Label art

# MICHAEL KERN

Kern Kalligraphie
www.kalligraphie-kern.de
seit 1989/Stuttgart

*Kalligraphie*

**Calligraphy is always different.
Every time.**

To write lettering, to create letters
– by hand, readable, beautiful,
surprising, lively, both well
thought-out and spontaneous,
aesthetic, artistic, balanced,
graceful, skilled, perfect.

Calligraphy comes in many forms
and expressions. It changes
constantly and every stroke is
new. The origins of calligraphy are
always determined by the artist
holding the feather. It is personal,
lively, magical. Writing is culture.
Handwriting is exclusive and com-
municates style.

**The written word is both substance and form. The
calligraher combines both in a well balanced unity.**

Das geschriebene Wort ist
Inhalt und Bild zugleich
Der Kalligraph vereint beides zu
einem harmonischen Ganzen

# Quittenbrot

PÂTE DE COINGS

Eines der ersten französischen
Rezepte für Quittenbrot (cotignac),
das die Stadt Orléans später zu
ihrer Spezialität gemacht hat.

2 kg reife Quitten
1 Liter Rotwein
½ kg Honig
½ TL Zimt
½ TL Ingwerpulver

Quitten schälen, entkernen
und in Stücke schneiden.
Mit Rotwein bedeckt langsam zum Kochen bringen. So lange kochen, bis die Quitten
weich sind. Abtropfen, durch ein Sieb streichen, bis man ein schönes Püree hat.
Auf 500 gr. Quittenpüree kommen 300 gr. abgekochter und abgeschäumter Honig.
Beides auf kleiner Flamme kochen, bis die Mischung eingekocht ist und eine
schöne, durchsichtige Paste bildet.
Am Schluss Gewürze untermischen. 1½ Zentimeter dick auf eine
Platte ausgießen und einige Tage trocknen lassen. In Rauten
schneiden und in Kristallzucker wälzen

**Handwriten script combined with illustration. The drawing is made a similar calligraphic penstroke, similar to that used for the writing.**

**This signet is a calligraphic word/figurative mark designed specifically for an anniversary celebration. From the dashed idea to the vectorized final artwork.**

**The gold lettering is set into the leather box, which contains historical art prints of zodiac signs. The calligraphy appears lavish and secretive.**

Die zwölf Tierkreiszeichen
und ihre Mythen

MR. KONE ® WEAR
*SINCE 1972*

YOUR

★HECHO EN MÉXICO

SINCE 1972★

**MR. KONE**
IS A STUDIO
OF GRAPHIC
DESIGN AND VISUAL
EXPERIMENTATION
FOUNDED
IN MEXICO
CITY.

**MR. KONE**
THEIR WORK
IS A MIX
OF IDEAS
AND
PERSONAL
PREFER-
ENCES.

**MR. KONE**
IS THE
PSEUDONYM
OF MEXICAN
GRAPHIC DESIGNER
CÉSAR
EVANGELISTA
BAUTISTA.

**MR. KONE**
USED IN
THEIR WORK
FUNNY
AND
IRONIC
CHARACTERS.

**MR. KONE**
IS LOOKING
FOR
CUSTOMERS THAT
TAKE
RISKS AND LIKE
EXPERIMENTING.

**MR. KONE**
BELIEVES
IN THE DREAMS
AND EVERYDAY
WORKS
TO MAKE
THEM COME
TRUE.

MR. KONE★

**MR. KONE**
HAS
WORKED
FOR BRANDS LIKE
MTV, NICKELODEON
NIKE, ADIDAS,
COCA-COLA,

PEPSI,
LIPTON
EUROPE, BRISK
USA, MINI COOPER
AND
INDEPENDENT
BRANDS.

*Mr. Kone*

MR. KONE
SINCE
1972
TRADEMARK
WWW.MRKONE.COM.MX

# Designers' Index

# Imprint

The Deutsche Nationalbibliothek
lists this publication in the
Deutsche Nationalbibliografie;
detailed bibliographic data are
available in the Internet at
http://dnb.dnb.de

ISBN 978-3-03768-163-3
© 2014 by Braun Publishing AG
www.braun-publishing.ch

1st edition 2014

Coordination:
Editorial office van Uffelen
Layout: the designers themselves
Text editing: Lisa Rogers, Clara
Vogel, Chris van Uffelen
Graphic concept: Michaela Prinz